Quilt
with
confidence

Nancy Zieman

Published by

krause publications

An Imprint of F+W Publications

700 East State Street • Iola, WI 54990-0001
715-445-2214 • 888-457-2873
www.krausebooks.com

Our toll-free number to place an order or obtain
a free catalog is (800) 258-0929.

Library of Congress Control Number: 2007940805

ISBN-13: 978-0-89689-593-5

ISBN-10: 0-89689-593-9

Designed by Laure Noe

Lead Editor: Pat Hahn

Editor: Diane Dhein

Printed in China

12 11 10 09   6 5 4 3

Contents

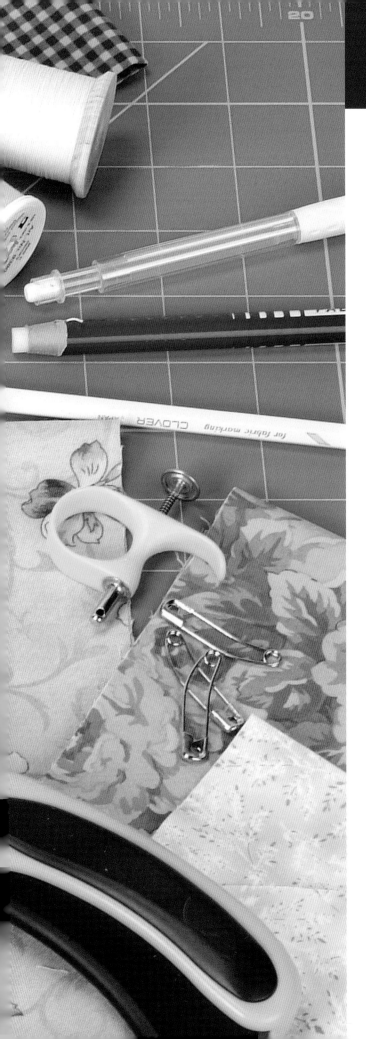

chapter 1

Quilting Quick Start

A new or wannabee quilter needs to know the basics of quilting—choosing and coordinating fabrics, selecting batting, gathering the most essential tools, and setting up an ergonomic and efficient work area. The following pages contain the information needed for an enlightening quilting experience. Learn the basics, and a unique quilting project is just around the corner!

Choosing the Right Fabric

It's time to quilt! Unless you use a kit that includes the fabric for your project, you'll need to select some fabrics. You'll want to consider quality, color schemes and fabric combinations, fabric design, and fabric care. Your completed project is bound to have more appeal when you do some planning!

Choosing fabric for your designs—that's the amazing part of quilting! Whether you are shopping for new fabric or delving into your precious stash, you'll find an overwhelming assortment of beautiful prints and colors. Consider the following guidelines when deciding which fabric is right for your project:

Quality

100% cotton is the traditional fabric choice for most quilting. It is very durable, and it holds a crease well. Holding a pressed crease will help define your patchwork lines and control points and curves on appliqué pieces. Good-quality fabric tends to be colorfast, and it is usually treated to resist wrinkling and soil.

Color Selection (Hue)

You don't need to be an artist to choose colors for your quilting project, but you do need to understand how colors relate to each other. Be creative—there isn't a wrong choice. There are, however, a few practical pointers for using color that will help you create the best designs.

Value

The value of a color is the amount of lightness or darkness that a color has. Adding white to a color produces a tint, and adding black gives the color a shade. Value creates illusions of movement and depth in your quilt. Some of the most attractive quilts include light, medium, and dark values.

If you have a difficult time determining a color's value, use a "value finder," which is made of clear red plastic. Look through it when viewing fabrics for value because it subtracts the color from the fabric and allows you to see only the value. The value finder helps you decide whether your fabrics are light, medium, or dark values. It is best to have a green value finder too, because the red one does not work on red fabrics. The value of a fabric depends on its own lightness or darkness plus the fabrics that surround it. A medium color may look light when placed with darks, or it may look dark when placed with lights.

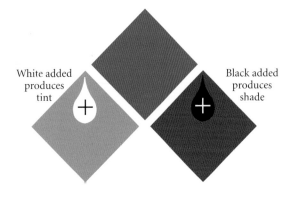

White added produces tint

Black added produces shade

Intensity

The brightness or dullness of a color is referred to as its intensity. You change intensity by adding grey or the color's complement (directly across from it on the color wheel).

In a harmonious color combination the fabrics have the same intensity. If one of the colors is too bright, the color scheme doesn't balance. For example, if you add a bright neon green to a primitive quilt with duller colorations it would signal the "color disaster team"! This doesn't mean that you can't mix different intensities. It simply suggests that a more intense color should be used in a smaller space so that it isn't overpowering.

Add grey to change intensity

Color Schemes and Fabric Combinations

- **Color Wheel Based:**

  A color wheel has twelve colors including the primary colors of yellow, red, and blue. The remaining colors on the wheel are obtained by mixing these three colors.

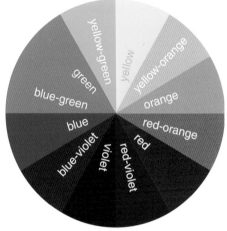

Monochromatic Schemes are tints and shades of one color such as light blue, medium blue, and navy blue. Tints of a color are those that have varying degrees of white added to them. In this instance light blue would be a tint of blue. Shades have varying degrees of black added to them. Navy blue is a shade of blue. Monochromatic schemes tend to be quiet and soothing. However, as a whole quilt, they may be a bit boring unless you vary the size of the prints used.

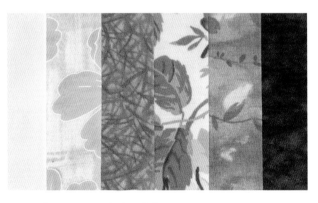

Analogous (similar or related) Color Schemes are colors that are next to each other on the color wheel, such as yellows, greens, and blues. Tints and shades of these colors make a very pleasing arrangement. Or, choose a color directly across from one of these colors as an accent.

Complementary Color Schemes use colors that are across from each other on the color wheel, such as yellow and violet. Complementary colors make each other seem more intense and bright.

Warm colors such as yellow, orange, and red are on one side of the color wheel, while cool colors such as blue, green, and violet are on the other side. Remember that warm colors advance and cool colors recede as you make your choices. Too many warm colors can be overpowering, just as too many cool colors can be boring. Neutral colors such as grey or cream work well with complementary color schemes and give the eye a place to pause.

Fabric Design

It is important to create visual texture in your quilt. This isn't a texture that you can feel with your hands, but one that is conceived by a combination of prints, solids, and colors. As you look at a quilt you should get a sense of a variety of textures that enhance one another. The size of the print that you choose, the placement of solids, and the intensity of the colors will definitely vary the visual texture.

Whether you are choosing fabrics based on a color scheme or starting with a focal fabric, the basic steps in choosing coordinating fabrics are the same.

- Choose small-, medium-, and large-scale prints to coordinate with your color scheme or focal fabric. These fabrics might include dots, florals, geometrics, stripes, paisleys, or any other prints that create a pleasing variety.

- **Colors Based on Fabric Themes:**
Here's another way to choose color. It's definitely the easiest method, since a designer has already completed the beautiful color scheme! Simply choose a "focal fabric" that is inspiring—one that you can't live without! Stand back about six feet from the fabric and see what colors "pop." Choose fabrics that coordinate, blend, or match the initial focal fabric.

- **Colors Based on Nature Schemes:**
Take a hike and view the awesome color inspiration in nature. Leaves, trees, flowers, animals, and more create natural color combinations.

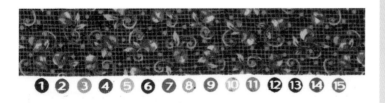

> ■ **NOTE FROM NANCY**
> *Check the selvages of your favorite fabric. Many designers print color swatches on the selvage for each of the colors used in the fabric. Use these printed swatches to select fabric colors that coordinate.*

- Arrange prints by size, including small, medium, and large prints.

- Include light-, medium-, and dark-value colors.

- Audition colors and prints for your quilt by laying your choices next to each other to see how they look. If you are auditioning bolts of fabric, stack them so that you are looking at their edges. Stand back about six to ten feet to see how well they coordinate.

Fabric Care

Wash or not? That question has been disputed by quilters for many years. Here are some points to ponder when you are trying to decide if washing your fabric before use is right for you, or not.

- Shrinkage:
  - **Yes, Wash it:** Prewashing reduces the likelihood of shrinkage after your quilt is complete.
  - **No, Don't wash it:** Shrinkage is usually minimal in good-quality fabric. A small amount of shrinkage may actually help hide machine quilting stitches.
- Fabric Finish:
  - **Yes, Wash it:** Many hand quilters like to wash their fabric before sewing it because it removes chemicals and gives the fabric a softer hand.
  - **No, Don't wash it:** Quilters who piece by machine usually like their fabric to feel stiffer. It is much easier to sew on. If they do prewash their fabric they may spray-starch the pieces before quilting them.
  - **No, Don't wash it:** The fabric is more prone to soiling when the finish is removed.

Choosing the Right Fabric

- **Colorfastness**
  - If you are washing your quilt, remember that detergent draws more dye out of fabric than a mild soap. Use a mild soap made especially for quilting, such as Orvus. Some manufacturers recommend baby shampoo, which is also a soap.

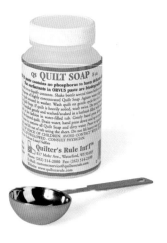

  - The best way to test your fabric for colorfastness and bleeding is to wash swatches of the darkest- and lightest-colored fabrics for your quilt together. If the dark fabric is not colorfast it will bleed onto the lighter fabric.

  - Prewashing your fabric does not necessarily mean that the dye will not run the second time the fabric is washed. Fabric that is prone to run will continue to do so with each washing.

  - One preventive measure that is recommended by many quilters is to use a product called Synthrapol. Synthrapol is a laundry additive that gets rid of the excess dye so that it doesn't bleed the next time the fabric is washed. Check with your local quilt shop or on the Internet to find this product.

  - Retayne is a product used to set dye. It is used primarily on fabrics that you *know* will fade when washed (such as deep reds and deep purples). Check with your local quilt shop or on the Internet to find this product.

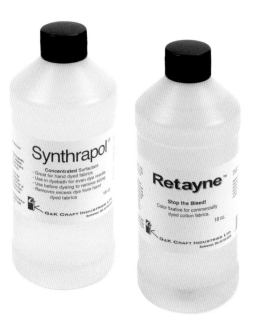

Batting

Batting gives a quilt loft (thickness). In general, the more loft a batting has, the warmer the quilt will be. Low-loft or thin batting is ideal for hand and machine quilting and for quilted garments. High-loft batting is primarily used for tied quilts and comforters. The thicker the batting, the more difficult it is to quilt by machine. Whatever thickness you plan to use, choose a good-quality batting with an even loft.

Many battings can now be purchased in white or black. Black is perfect to use for quilts with a dark quilt top and backing.

High-loft batting

Low-loft batting

Thin batting

Black batting

Choosing Batting

Batting Choices

Polyester batts:

- are easy to stitch through
- do not breathe as well as natural fiber batts
- are available in several different weights and are often listed by the number of ounces per yard

Note: Use a batt with a weight no heavier than 10 oz. for machine quilting. Heavier weights are suited for hand tying, but are too thick for machine quilting.

- are preferred by many for wall hangings, because several are thin and lightweight
- have greater loft than cotton, so quilts are puffy
- are inexpensive
- are washable and have very little shrinkage
- have a tendency to beard

Note: Unless the surface of polyester batting is treated in some way, fibers can beard, or work their way to the surface of the quilted project. Some batts are thermal bonded to prevent bearding: Heat melts a portion of the fibers to serve as a natural bonding. Other batts have a scrim, a backing on both sides that prevents fibers from migrating to the surface.

Needle punch scrim

Cotton batts:

- are lightweight, soft, and drape well
- have low loft
- are easy to quilt by machine
- are a good choice for beginning quilters
- are reasonably priced
- are washed in cold water to prevent shrinkage

Cotton/polyester blend batts:

- give you the ease of quilting by hand or machine, plus have a more traditional appearance
- are less likely to beard
- are warmer and heavier than polyester batting with the same loft
- are reasonably priced
- are washed in cold water to prevent shrinkage (follow manufacturer's instructions)

Wool batts:

- are warm, light, and wonderful to touch
- drape well and are easy to machine or hand quilt
- have a slight tendency to beard
- are more costly
- are dry-cleaned to prevent shrinkage and matting

Silk batts:

- drape well
- can be sticky to stitch through
- may beard through cotton fabrics
- are warm and lightweight
- are more costly
- are dry-cleaned or delicately washed according to manufacturer's instructions

Machine Quilting Specifications

Natural-fiber batts (cotton and wool) need to be quilted closer together than those of synthetic fibers (polyester). Always check the manufacturer's specifications to see what the manufacturer recommends. The following are guidelines:

- Quilt cotton and wool batts every 1"–2" so the fibers don't separate and bunch up.
- Quilt polyester batts every 4"–6". The needle slides easily through a polyester batt.

Essential Quilting Tools

There is a plethora of quilting tools available! Add time-saving quilting notions to your collection as you take on new quilting challenges. These essentials will get you started with basic quilting.

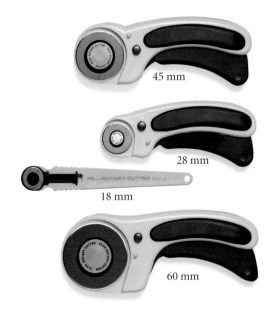

45 mm

28 mm

18 mm

60 mm

● **Rotary Cutters:** A rotary cutter works much like a pizza cutter, but it has a razor-sharp blade that cuts fabric with ease. Remember to retract the blade after each use to protect yourself and others. Keep the cutter out of the reach of children.

- A variety of sizes are available; however, the most widely used is the 45 mm. It is large enough to cut through several layers of fabric without undue stress.
- Smaller cutters, such as the 28 mm and 18 mm, are helpful for cutting around templates and patterns.
- Large cutters, such as the 60 mm cutter, are very helpful when cutting lofty fabrics such as fleece or wool.

● **Cutting Mat:** A cutting mat is a necessity when using a rotary cutter.

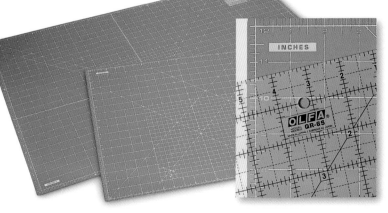

- A mat protects your tabletop or floor.
- Grid marks provide handy reference points for measuring and cutting.
- Mats grip fabric to prevent sliding as you cut.
- The self-healing ability of a cutting mat assures longevity with normal use.
- Multiple sizes are available for quilting convenience and efficiency.

NOTE FROM NANCY

The 18" x 24" mat is the basic size. Many quilters have numerous mats. Yet as a beginner, the 18" x 24" mat is the most efficient for cutting strips of 41"– 45" wide quilting fabric.

● **Ruler:** A see-through acrylic ruler provides accurate measurements and a straight edge for cutting.

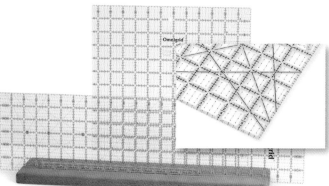

- A 6½" x 24" ruler is a convenient size for quilting.
- Choose a laser-cut ruler that has marked ⅛" increments for the greatest cutting accuracy.
- It is helpful to have a ruler with marked 30°, 45° and 60° angles.
- Other specialty rulers are available for specific quilting projects.

Shears/Scissors: Shears have one large hole for fingers and a smaller hole for your thumb. The blades of shears can be either straight or bent and are more than 6" long. A scissors has two finger holes the same size, and the blades are less than 6" long.

- Use a good-quality shears for cutting fabric. An 8" knife-edge, bent dressmaker shears is an excellent choice.
- An inexpensive pair of shears or scissors is fine for cutting template plastic, batting, and appliqués with paper-backed fusible webbing attached.
- A good sharp pair of scissors, such as the 5" Tailor's Points and Craft Scissors, is handy for cutting threads and trimming around curves and in small places.

NOTE FROM NANCY

My "sharp advice" would be to buy the best shears or scissors you can afford. Your hands will definitely thank you as you create that new quilt!

Thread: Good quality thread is essential, especially if you want your project to become a family heirloom. Remember that old thread can become brittle and break as you are quilting, or even worse, after you have finished the quilt!

- For machine piecing use cotton or cotton covered polyester thread.
- For machine quilting use matching cotton thread, or monofilament thread that is thin and soft.

Needles:

Hand quilting needles:
- Although we present minimal hand quilting techniques in this book, a "betweens" size 10 is generally preferred for hand quilting. You might want to start with a size 9 if you have never hand quilted before, and increase the size to 10 or 11 as you become more proficient. The larger the number, the smaller the needle.
- A "sharp" needle is a little longer and has a larger eye. This needle is used most commonly for hand basting.

Machine quilting needles:
- A machine quilting needle sews through the thick layers and intersections of crossed seams in quilting or patchwork. Compared to a universal needle, a machine quilting needle has a specially tapered ultra-sharp point and extra-stiff shaft to provide better stitch quality and control on multiple layers of fabric.

universal

machine quilting

Organizing the Quilting Area

After you've selected fabrics and purchased quilting supplies, it's time to organize your quilting area. Provide space for cutting/design, sewing, and pressing. Arrange those areas in a triangle for greatest efficiency.

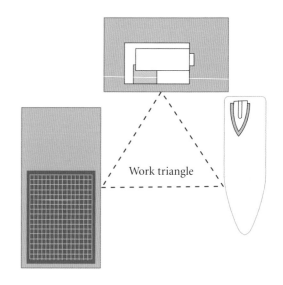

Work triangle

- Store tools together and in or close to the area in which they are used. See-through containers, open baskets, or drawers work well for storage.
  - **Cutting/Design Area:** Store rotary cutters, rulers, large cutting mats, markers, templates, and graph paper.
  - **Sewing Area:** Store thread, presser feet, pins, and scissors/shears.
  - **Pressing Area:** Store iron, spray starch, water for iron, pressing sheets and cloths, and pins.

- Keep the work triangle small to shorten the distance needed to complete the job.

Ruler and mat storage

Sewing supply storage

Pressing storage

Storage Organization

- **Books:**
  - Group books by similar topics.

- **Projects:**
  - Store unfinished projects in a labeled box with all of the components necessary for completion.
  - Place photos, fabric swatches, or drawings on the outside of the box to help jog your memory about what's stored inside.

- **Fabrics:**
  - Organize fabrics by color and value to help determine which you need to replace on your next fabric buying trip.
  - Store folded fabric on shelving 14"–16" deep.
  - Consider adding doors on your fabric storage area if it receives a lot of sun to reduce fabric fading.

Fabric storage

Ergonomics

- **Lighting:**
  - Good room lighting is important 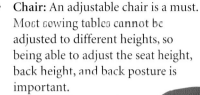—have as much natural light as possible.
  - Choose task lighting using lamps with true color light bulbs such as the Ott-Lite®. True color lighting is not only a brighter option and less tiring for your eyes, but also helps you match colors more accurately. Consider task lighting for each area of the work triangle.

- **Machine:**
  - Align your body with the sewing machine needle. Allow leg room on both sides of your machine.

Center your body in front of needle

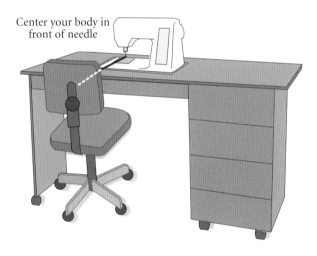

  - The best countertop height for sewing is 28".
  - Many quilters tilt their machines forward using a platform such as the Tilt'able™ for more comfort.

- **Chair:** An adjustable chair is a must. Most sewing tables cannot be adjusted to different heights, so being able to adjust the seat height, back height, and back posture is important.
  - Adjust the seat of the chair so that your palms rest on the machine table. Your relaxed arms and shoulders should form a 90° angle.
  - Allow approximately 9" from your machine table to the seat of your chair for a person with an average torso length.
  - Adjust the back of the chair for good lumbar support and back posture.

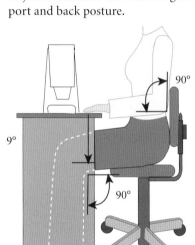

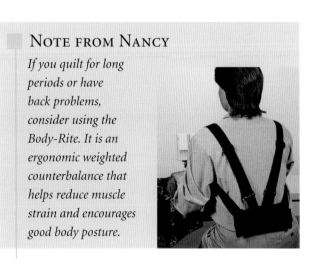

NOTE FROM NANCY

If you quilt for long periods or have back problems, consider using the Body-Rite. It is an ergonomic weighted counterbalance that helps reduce muscle strain and encourages good body posture.

- **Cutting Table:**
  - 36" is an ideal cutting height for most average size adults. This is the height of most kitchen countertops. To determine the proper height for you, measure the distance from your elbow to the ground when you are standing with your shoulders relaxed—the cutting surface should be 6" lower than this measurement.

▊ NOTE FROM NANCY

If you are tall consider raising your work table with large cans of tomato juice. It works well for me.

  - A toe kick that allows you to stand with your toes slightly underneath, as on kitchen cabinets, makes standing for long periods of time much more comfortable.

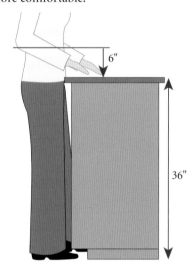

- **Ironing Board:**
  - Pressing while standing: Adjust ironing board about 3" higher than your cutting table height.
  - Pressing while sitting: Adjust pressing surface a few inches lower than your machine bed.
  - Place a quick press area perpendicular rather than parallel to your machine.
  - Built-in ironing boards take up less floor space and can be folded up and out of sight when not in use. However, the surface area is limited if you plan to use it for your regular pressing as well.

▊ NOTE FROM NANCY

A great makeshift ironing surface for a tall quilter is a padded door placed over your washer and dryer.

- **Pattern Storage:** Slip patterns in clear plastic sheet protectors and store them in notebooks or office file drawers, shoe boxes, or magazine organizers.

- **Design Wall:** Fabric pieces stick to a flannel Design Wall without pinning so that large quilt pieces can be arranged with ease. Place the Design Wall behind a door for most efficient use of space. This Design Wall doesn't interfere with the door swing.

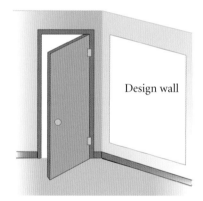

The Design Layout Sheet is easy to hang, the fabrics stay in place, and the sheet can be folded up to transport or store your designs.

The Ideal Compact Sewing Area

If you have limited space for your quilting area try to include some of the following features.

- Cabinet or sturdy table and chair for your sewing machine work area, with ample leg room and ergonomic features discussed on page 15.
- Drawer and cupboard space to store quilting supplies for each area of the work triangle. A multitude of storage space yields an area that is clutter free when not in use.
- Cutting space that can accommodate a smaller mat for quickly cutting small projects, but can open up to a larger surface for cutting or working on larger quilted projects.
- Ironing surface for fast pressing without having to set up a large ironing board.
- Additional lighting that can be moved to various areas as needed.
- Design Wall for laying out blocks to find the best possible combinations. Lower your machine into a cabinet if possible to create additional work space for designing. A laptop computer with quilting software is a quilter's dream for this designing area!

chapter 2

Simplify with Strips and Strata

Cutting hundreds of individual patchwork pieces can be a thing of the past when you use strips and strata! In this chapter you will learn to make several popular blocks in different sizes. I also detail strategies for combining various blocks. The techniques are fast and fun—create a simple quilt with ease!

Basics for Preparing Strata

Stratas are the basis for many patchwork designs. Rotary cut fabric into strips, stitch the strips together to form stratas, and then subcut them into sections. This saves time, increases accuracy, and eliminates the need for templates.

Basic Rotary Cutting: Fabric into Strips

1 Prepare fabric for cutting.

- Fold fabric in half, meeting selvage edges.

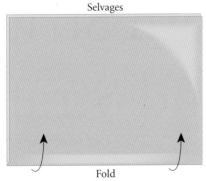

Selvages

Fold

- Fold fabric again, bringing the fold to the selvages. (There now will be four layers of fabric.)

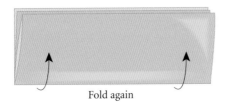

Fold again

- Place the fabric on a rotary cutting mat, aligning the fold along one of the horizontal lines at the lower edge of the mat.

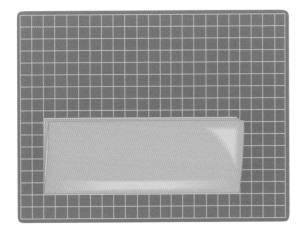

- Position a ruler on the fabric perpendicular to the fold so it forms a right angle. Straighten fabric edge using a rotary cutter to trim away any excess fabric.

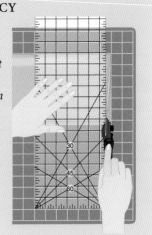

NOTE FROM NANCY

For greatest accuracy, I prefer to have the majority of the fabric to the left of the ruler when I make that first cut to straighten the edge. Firmly hold the ruler in position with your left hand, and cut with your right. Then carefully rotate the mat so the trimmed edge of the fabric is on the left before cutting the strips.

2 Cut strips.

Note: Throughout this book we use 3½", 6½", and 12½" blocks. Those measurements allow for ¼" seam allowances on all outer edges. With each specific block design, you'll be given the exact strip sizes to cut. These BASIC instructions give an overview of the process.

- Determine strip width. The width of the strip is determined by the completed design.

- Align one of the ruler's horizontal lines with the fabric fold. Working from the straightened edge, place the line corresponding to the desired strip width along the straightened edge of the fabric.

- Cut fabric into crosswise strips.

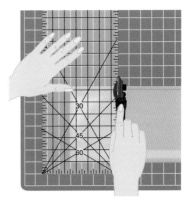

Basic Block Size

Use a 3½", 6½", or 12½" block size for any of the styles in this book you are inspired to make. No additional math is required—the combinations will fit together.

12½" block

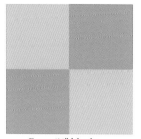

Four 6½" blocks =
one 12½" block

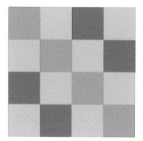

Sixteen 3½" blocks =
one 12½" block

Basic Stitching: Strips into Strata

1 Stack strips, placing all strips of one color in one stack.

2 Form strip groupings, according to the completed block design.

3 Stitch strips into stratas.
- Set stitch length at 2.5 (12–15 stitches per inch), slightly shorter than normal. Because strips will be recut, a shorter stitch length makes stitching more secure.
- Join edges with ¼" seams, right sides together.

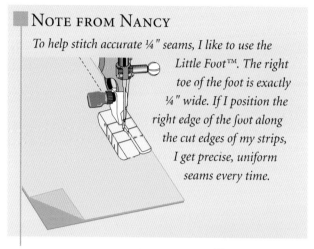

NOTE FROM NANCY

To help stitch accurate ¼" seams, I like to use the Little Foot™. The right toe of the foot is exactly ¼" wide. If I position the right edge of the foot along the cut edges of my strips, I get precise, uniform seams every time.

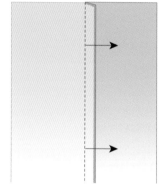

4 Press seams in one direction, generally toward the darker fabric.

Basic Strata Cutting: Strata into Sections

1 Straighten the edge of the strata. Align one edge of the seamed strata along one of the horizontal markings on the cutting mat. Align one of the ruler's horizontal markings with the cut edge of the strata.

2 Cut stratas into sections.

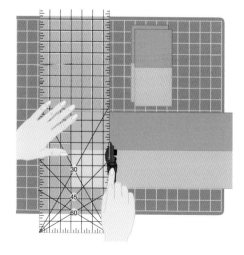

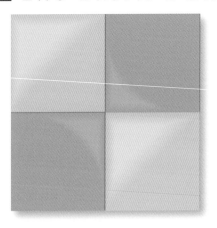

Create 4-patch units using this easy strip-piecing method without cutting any square shapes! We have included several options for you to try. Make sure to sketch them out or cut and arrange squares of fabric—the way they are positioned affects the design you achieve.

The two-fabric option is the easiest to start with. Once you have the 4-patch technique down pat, then it is time to mix up the colors or fabrics!

Note: All seams are ¼" unless otherwise stated.

Select Fabrics

1 Select two contrasting or coordinating fabrics.

2 Label one Fabric A, and the other Fabric B.

Block Size (Includes ¼" seam allowances on all edges.)
- 12½" finished block: Cut crosswise strips 6½" wide.
- 6½" finished block: Cut crosswise strips 3½" wide.
- 3½" finished block: Cut crosswise strips 2" wide.

Cut Fabric into Strips

1 Cut at least one crosswise strip of Fabric A.

2 Cut at least one crosswise strip of Fabric B.

Stitch Strips into Strata

For a two-color block, form one strata using strips of two different fabrics.

1 Join the lengthwise edges of Fabric A and Fabric B strips, right sides together, using ¼" seams.

> **■ NOTE FROM NANCY**
> *If you are making more than one strata, do not raise the presser foot or cut the threads after completing the seam. "Kiss" the second set of strips to the first and continue sewing, chain piecing the strips together.*

2 Press seams toward the darker fabric.

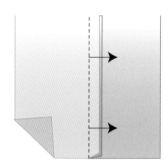

3 When working with a single strata, meet short ends of the strata. Cut strata in half, making two pieces, each approximately 21" long.

4 Arrange the strata in two stacks that are mirror images of each other. One strata will have Fabric A on top, and the other will have Fabric B on top.

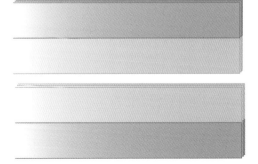

Subcut Strata and Complete Blocks

1 Straighten the edge of each strata as detailed on p. 20, aligning the ruler's horizontal markings with the cut edge of the strips.

2 Stack one of each strata with right sides together as shown, stacking and aligning the straight edges and seams as perfectly as possible. Fabric A will be on top of one strata and Fabric B on top of the other.

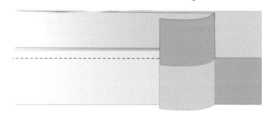

3 Subcut strata sections the same width as the original strip width. For example, when using 3½" strips, cut sections 3½" wide. Keep the subcuts in pairs, so the pairs are ready for stitching.

Original strip width

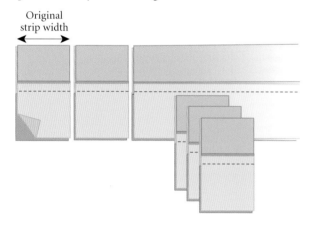

4 Chain stitch the pairs, right sides together, to create blocks, aligning seam intersections. Stitch lengthwise edges of one pair, then "kiss" a second pair to the first and continue stitching. Repeat until all pairs are joined.

5 Clip threads to separate blocks.

6 Press seams flat, then to one side.

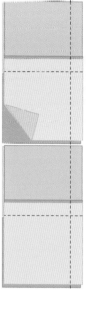

■ NOTE FROM NANCY

Pressing the strata seam allowances toward the darker fabric each time makes it easier to precisely meet the seamlines when assembling larger blocks.

COLOR CONFIDENCE

Now that you know how to make a 4-Patch block, try using several of those blocks to create a design. Adding solid colored blocks between 4-Patch blocks adds interest and variety. Changing the color or position of blocks gives a totally different look. What fun!

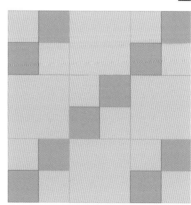

Three-Fabric 4-Patch

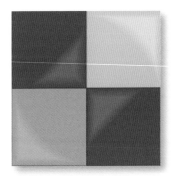

Note: All seams are ¼" unless otherwise stated.

Select Fabrics

1 Select three contrasting or coordinating fabrics.

2 Label one Fabric A, one Fabric B, and the other Fabric C.

> **NOTE FROM NANCY**
> It's important that both light and dark fabrics are used to create a traditional 4-patch. In the illustrated 3-fabric option, the two dark strips are Fabric A, and the light strips are Fabrics B and C.

Block Size (Includes ¼" seam allowances on all edges.)

- 12½" finished block: Cut crosswise strips 6½" wide.
- 6½" finished block: Cut crosswise strips 3½" wide.
- 3½" finished block: Cut crosswise strips 2" wide.

Cut Fabric into Strips

1 Cut two crosswise strips of Fabric A.

2 Cut one crosswise strip each of Fabric B and Fabric C.

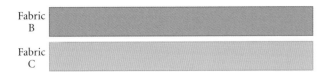

Stitch Strips into Strata

1 Strata 1: Join one Fabric A strip and one Fabric B strip into a strata, right sides together. Press seam toward darker fabric.

2 Strata 2: Join the second Fabric A strip and the Fabric C strip, right sides together. Press seam toward darker fabric.

Subcut Strata and Complete Blocks

1 Straighten the edge of each strata as detailed on p. 20, aligning the ruler's horizontal markings with the cut edge of the strips.

2 Stack the strata with right sides together, stacking and aligning the straight edges and seams as perfectly as possible.

3 Subcut strata sections the same width as the original strip size. For example, when using 3½" strips, cut sections 3½" wide. Keep the subcuts in pairs so they are ready for stitching.

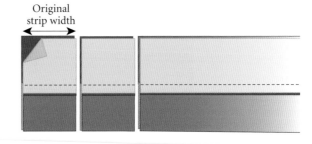

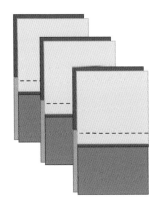

4 Chain stitch the pairs, right sides together, to create blocks, aligning seam intersections. Stitch lengthwise edges of one pair, then "kiss" a second pair to the first and continue stitching. Repeat until all pairs are joined.

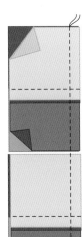

5 Clip threads to separate blocks.

6 Press seams flat, then to one side.

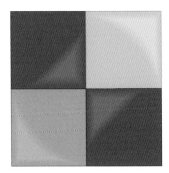

What a difference changing colorations and block arrangements makes! Take a look at these options alternating 4-patch blocks with solid blocks. Now take squares of fabric and arrange them to create your own adaptation.

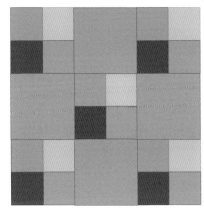

Four-Fabric 4-Patch

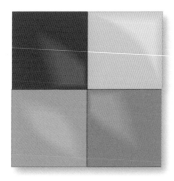

Note: All seams are ¼" unless otherwise stated.

Select Fabrics

1 Select four contrasting or coordinating fabrics.

2 Label one Fabric A, one Fabric B, one Fabric C, and the other Fabric D.

> ### NOTE FROM NANCY
> *It is important that there are two dark and two light colors in the 4-fabric option. Color makes all the difference! In our example the two dark strips are Fabrics A and D, and the light strips are Fabrics B and C.*

Block Size (Includes ¼" seam allowances on all edges.)

- 12½" finished block: Cut crosswise strips 6½" wide.
- 6½" finished block: Cut crosswise strips 3½" wide.
- 3½" finished block: Cut crosswise strips 2" wide.

Cut Fabric into Strips

Cut one crosswise strip each of Fabrics A, B, C, and D.

Stitch Strips into Strata

1 Strata 1: Join Fabric A and Fabric B strips, right sides together. Press seam toward darker fabric.

2 Strata 2: Join Fabric C and Fabric D strips, right sides together. Press seam toward darker fabric.

Subcut Strata and Complete Blocks

1 Straighten the edge of each strata as detailed on p. 20, aligning the ruler's horizontal markings with the cut edge of the strips.

2 Stack the stratas with right sides together, stacking and aligning the straight edges and seams as perfectly as possible.

3 Subcut strata sections the same width as the original strip size. For example, when using 3½" strips, cut sections 3½" wide. Keep the subcuts in pairs so they are ready for stitching.

Original strip width

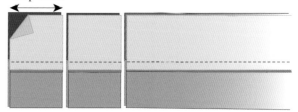

4 Chain stitch the pairs, right sides together, to create blocks, aligning seam intersections. Stitch lengthwise edges of one pair, then "kiss" a second pair to the first and continue stitching. Repeat until all pairs are joined.

5 Clip threads to separate blocks.

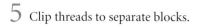

6 Press seams flat, then to one side.

COLOR CONFIDENCE

Now it's time to play with colorations and block arrangements. Change the colors of the strips and/or the order in which they are joined. Then combine solid blocks with 4-patch blocks to create a wealth of variations. You're totally in charge.

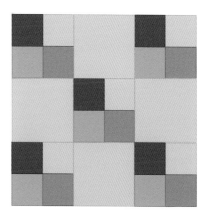

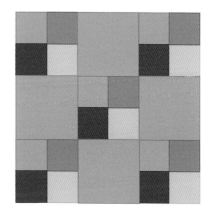

Two-Fabric 9-Patch Blocks

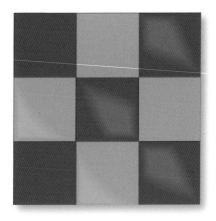

Many creative projects start with 9-patch blocks. Vary the strip width, fabric, and layout for a potpourri of expressive quilt blocks. Trivets, potholders, pillows, wall hangings, quilts, and more can be created with the same block, using different strip widths.

Note: All seams are ¼" unless otherwise stated.

Select Fabrics

1 Select two contrasting or coordinating fabrics.

2 Label one Fabric A, and the other Fabric B.

Block Size (Includes ¼" seam allowances on all edges.)

- 12½" finished block: Cut crosswise strips 4½" wide.
- 6½" finished block: Cut crosswise strips 2½" wide.
- 3½" finished block: Cut crosswise strips 1½" wide.

Cut Fabric into Strips

1 Cut three strips of Fabric A.

2 Cut three strips of Fabric B.

Stitch Strips into Strata

1 Form two groupings, each with three strips.
- Strata 1: Position the strips with one Fabric A strip in the center of two Fabric B strips.
- Strata 2: Position the strips with a Fabric B strip in the center of two Fabric A strips.

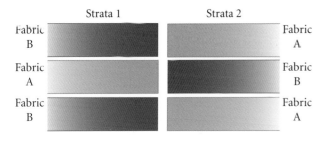

2 Join the three strips to form Strata 1.
- Join the lengthwise edges of one Fabric B strip to the Fabric A strip, right sides together.

- Join the lengthwise edges of the remaining Fabric B strip to the opposite edge of the Fabric A strip, right sides together.

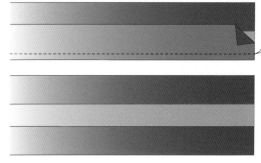

- If you are making more than one of the strata, do not raise the presser foot or cut the threads. "Kiss" the second set of strips to the first and continue sewing, chain piecing the strips together.
- Press seams toward the darker fabric.

3 Repeat, joining strips in Strata 2.

Subcut Strata and Complete Blocks

1 Straighten the edge of each strata as detailed on p. 20, aligning the ruler's horizontal markings with the cut edge of the strips.

2 Subcut strata sections the same width as the original strip size. For example, if the original strips were 4½" wide, cut the sections 4½" wide.

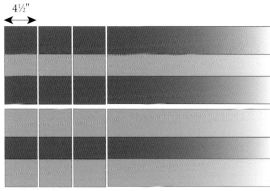

4½"

3 Separate cut sections into two groupings, with those of each strata together.

4 Chain stitch sections together. Use two Strata 1 sections and one Strata 2 section to complete one block.

Strata 1   Strata 2

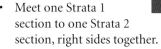

- Meet one Strata 1 section to one Strata 2 section, right sides together.
- Join the remaining Strata 1 section to the edge of Strata 2 as shown, to complete the 9-patch block. Press seams open.

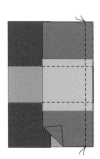 

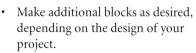

- Make additional blocks as desired, depending on the design of your project.

NOTE FROM NANCY

As an option, use two Strata 2 sections and one Strata 1 section to complete a block. Your block options are almost limitless!

COLOR CONFIDENCE

See what a difference changing the positions of the fabrics makes in the finished block. And, by changing the fabric of the solid-colored block you have even more options. Use the following combinations as a start to build your quilting confidence.

Note: All seams are ¼" unless otherwise stated.

Select Fabrics

1 Select three contrasting or coordinating fabrics.

2 Label one Fabric A, one Fabric B, and the other Fabric C.

Block Size (Includes ¼" seam allowances on all edges.)

- 12½" finished block: Cut crosswise strips 4½" wide.
- 6½" finished block: Cut crosswise strips 2½" wide.
- 3½" finished block: Cut crosswise strips 1½" wide.

Cut Fabric into Strips

1 Cut two crosswise strips of Fabric A.

2 Cut three crosswise strips of Fabric B.

3 Cut one crosswise strip of Fabric C.

Stitch Strips into Strata

1 Form two groupings, each with three strips.
- Strata 1: Position one each of Fabrics A, B, and C.
- Strata 2: Position two strips of Fabric B with one strip of Fabric A in the center.

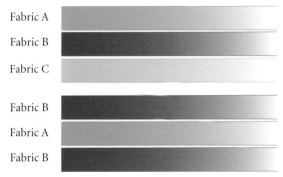

2 Join the three strips of each grouping together, forming two stratas.

Subcut Strata and Complete Blocks

1 Straighten the edge of each strata as detailed on p. 20, aligning the ruler's horizontal markings with the cut edge of the strips.

2 Subcut strata sections the same width as the original strip size. For example, if the original strips were 4½" wide, cut the sections 4½" wide.

3 Separate cut sections into three groups, with those of each strata together. Use two sections of the Strata 1 (one will be flipped), and one section of Strata 2 for one block.

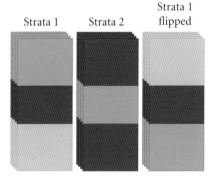

4 Chain stitch sections together.
- Meet and join one Strata 1 section to one Strata 2 section, right sides together. Repeat with additional Strata 1 and Strata 2 sections.

- Meet and join the remaining Strata 1 section to the edge of the Strata 2 section as shown, to complete the 9-patch block. Press seams open.

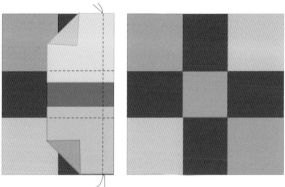

- Make additional blocks as desired, depending on the design of your project.

Four-Fabric 9-Patch

Note: All seams are ¼" unless otherwise stated.

Select Fabrics

1 Select four contrasting or coordinating fabrics.

2 Label one Fabric A, one Fabric B, one Fabric C, and one Fabric D.

Block Size (Includes ¼" seam allowances on all edges.)

- 12½" finished block: Cut crosswise strips 4½" wide.
- 6½" finished block: Cut crosswise strips 2½" wide.
- 3½" finished block: Cut crosswise strips 1½" wide.

Cut Fabric into Strips

1 Cut three crosswise strips of Fabric A.

2 Cut one crosswise strip of Fabric B.

3 Cut one crosswise strip of Fabric C.

4 Cut one crosswise strip of Fabric D.

Stitch Strips into Strata

1 Form two groupings, each with three strips.

> ### NOTE FROM NANCY
> *You could make many combinations of the four fabrics. Move and rearrange strips until you're pleased with the design. We show one possible arrangement to illustrate the process.*

- Strata 1: Position and join the strips with a Fabric A strip in the center, C on top, and D on the bottom.
- Strata 2: Position and join the strips with a Fabric B strip in the center of two Fabric A strips.

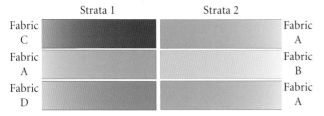

2 Press seams toward the darker fabric.

Subcut Strata and Complete Blocks

1 Straighten the edge of each strata as detailed on p. 20, aligning the ruler's horizontal markings with the cut edge of the strips.

2 Subcut strata sections the same width as the original strip size. For example, if the original strips were 4½" wide, cut the sections 4½" wide.

3 Separate cut sections into three groups, with those of each strata together. Use two sections of Strata 1 (one flipped) and one section of Strata 2 for one block.

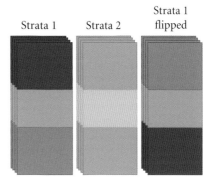

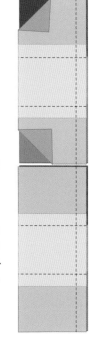

4 Chain stitch sections together.
- Meet and join one Strata 1 section to one Strata 2 section, right sides together. Repeat, with additional Strata 1 and Strata 2 sections.
- Join the flipped Strata 1 sections to the edges of the Strata 2 sections as shown, to complete 9-patch blocks.
- Make additional blocks as desired, depending on the design of your project.

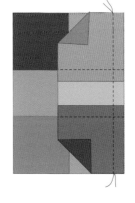

Scrappy Nine-Fabric 9-Patch

Note: All seams are ¼" unless otherwise stated.

Select Fabrics

1 Select nine contrasting or coordinating fabrics.

2 Label fabrics A–I.

Block Size (Includes ¼" seam allowances on all edges.)

- 12½" finished block: Cut crosswise strips 4½" wide.
- 6½" finished block: Cut crosswise strips 2½" wide.
- 3½" finished block: Cut crosswise strips 1½" wide.

Cut Fabric into Strips

1 Cut one strip each of nine different fabrics.

2 Label fabrics A–I.

Stitch Strips into Strata

1 Form three groupings, each with three strips.
- Strata 1: Use strips ABC.
- Strata 2: Use strips DEF.
- Strata 3: Use strips GHI.

2 Stitch strips of each grouping together, forming three stratas.
- Join the lengthwise edges of Strata 1 Fabrics ABC, right sides together.

Strata 1

| Fabric A |
| Fabric B |
| Fabric C |

- Join the lengthwise edges of Strata 2 Fabrics DEF, right sides together.

Strata 2

| Fabric D |
| Fabric E |
| Fabric F |

- Join the lengthwise edges of Strata 3 Fabrics GHI, right sides together.

Strata 3

| Fabric G |
| Fabric H |
| Fabric I |

3 Press seams toward the darker fabric.

Subcut Strata and Complete Blocks

1 Straighten the edge of each strata as detailed on p. 20, aligning the ruler's horizontal markings with the cut edge of the strips.

2 Subcut strata sections the same width as the original strip size. For example, if the original strips were 4½" wide, cut the sections 4½" wide.

3 Separate cut sections into three groupings, with those of each strata together. Use one section of Strata 1, one section of Strata 2, and one section of Strata 3 for each block.

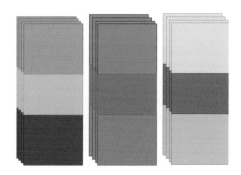

4 Chain stitch sections together.

- Meet and join one Strata 1 section to one Strata 2 section, right sides together. Repeat with additional Strata 1 and Strata 2 sections.

- Join the Strata 3 section to the edge of the Strata 2 section as shown, to complete the 9-patch block.

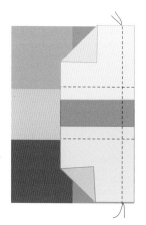

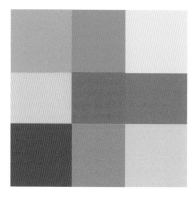

5 Make additional blocks as desired, depending on the design of your project.

COLOR CONFIDENCE

When you use multiple fabrics, the combinations are virtually endless. Here are a few to get you started. Enjoy playing with color and design with this basic quilt block.

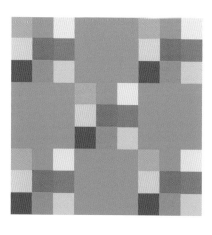

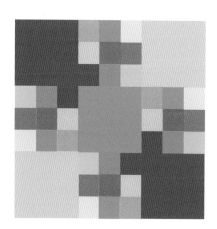

16-Patch Block

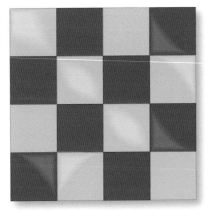

The key to creating a 16-patch block is sewing four strips together to make a strata. Subcut sections from the strata and stitch them together to form the 16-patch block. It's easy, and there are no little pieces to contend with.

Note: All seams are ¼" unless otherwise stated.

Select Fabrics

1 Select two fabrics—one light and one medium or dark.

2 Label one Fabric A, and the other Fabric B.

Block Size (Includes ¼" seam allowances on all edges.)

For a 12½" finished block: Cut crosswise strips 3½" wide.

Cut Fabric into Strips

1 Cut two 3½" crosswise strips of Fabric A.

2 Cut two 3½" crosswise strips of Fabric B.

Stitch Strips into Strata

1 Form one four-strip grouping, alternating two Fabric A and two Fabric B strips.

> ### NOTE FROM NANCY
> *It's easier to organize your strips if you arrange the rows on a terry towel. This also makes it easy to move them to the machine for stitching and to store them between quilting sessions.*

2 Join the four strips together, forming a strata, joining the lengthwise edges of fabrics with right sides together.

Fabric A
Fabric B
Fabric A
Fabric B

3 Press seams toward the darker fabric.

Subcut Strata and Complete Blocks

1 Straighten the edge of the strata as detailed on p. 20, aligning the ruler's horizontal markings with the cut edge of the strips.

2 Subcut each strata the same width as the original strip size. In this instance the original strips were 3½" wide, so cut the sections 3½" wide.

Original strip width

3 Separate the sections into two stacks that are mirror images of each other. One section will have Fabric A on the top, and the other will have Fabric B on the top.

4 Join four sections to form a block.
- Join sections into pairs.
  - Meet a section from each stack, right sides together. Stitch seam, matching seam intersections. Because seam allowances were pressed toward the darker fabric, the intersections will easily mesh together and align.
  - At the end of the seam, do not raise the presser foot or cut threads. "Kiss" a second set of sections to the first and continue stitching, chain stitching the sections together.
  - Repeat, chain stitching all sections into pairs if you plan to make more than one block. Then clip the threads between pairs to separate them.
  - Press seams flat, then to one side.

- Join pairs into one or more 16-patch blocks.
  - Arrange pairs in two stacks.

  - Meet a pair from each stack, right sides together. Join pairs to make 16-patch blocks.
  - Press seams flat, then to one side.

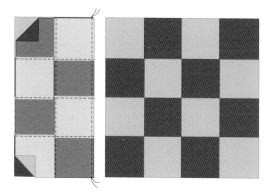

COLOR CONFIDENCE

As you become more confident in making 16-patch blocks, try using two different strata (three or more fabrics). It's a new look using the same stitching techniques! Our illustrations show the same strata used in rows 1 and 4, and rows 2 and 3, except they are mirror imaged.

Triple Rail Block

A Triple Rail (sometimes referred to as a Rail Fence) is a very easy block to complete—the finished block is complete after the first subcut! Simply make a three-strip strata for each block. Vary the size and fabric arrangement to achieve a contemporary look.

Select Fabrics

1 Select one light, one medium, and one dark fabric.

2 Label one Fabric A, one Fabric B, and the other Fabric C.

Block Size (Includes ¼" seam allowances on all edges.)

- 12½" finished block: Cut crosswise strips 4½" wide.
- 6½" finished block: Cut crosswise strips 2½" wide.
- 3½" finished block: Cut crosswise strips 1½" wide.

Cut Fabric into Strips

1 Cut one strip of Fabric A.

2 Cut one strip of Fabric B.

3 Cut one strip of Fabric C.

Stitch Strips into Strata

Note: All seams are ¼" unless otherwise stated.

1 Arrange the strips to form a strata as shown.

2 Join the strips together, right sides together, using ¼" seams.

3 Press seams toward the darker fabric.

Subcut Strata and Complete Blocks

1 Straighten the edge of the strata as detailed on p. 20, aligning the ruler's horizontal markings with the cut edge of the strips.

2 Cut the completed strata to the correct finished block size. For example, with 4½" strips, the finished block should measure 12½" square.

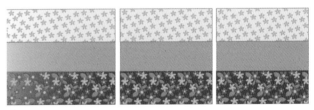

3 Arrange and join the blocks into rows to form a design.
- Arrange blocks in desired number of rows and columns.
- Alternate block positions, placing blocks so fabric strips run horizontally on one block and vertically on the adjacent block.

- Meet and join the first two blocks in row 1, right sides together. Do not cut threads.
- Meet the first two blocks in row 2. "Kiss" them to the blocks from row 1 and continue stitching.
- Continue, chain stitching remaining first and second blocks in each row into pairs. Then clip the threads between pairs to separate them. Press seams flat, then to one side.

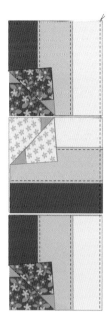

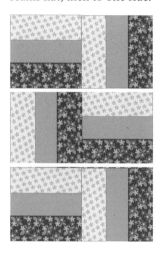

- Repeat, joining the next block in each row to the joined pairs, again chain stitching blocks together.
- Continue until all blocks for each row have been joined.

4 Join rows.
- Meet row 1 to row 2, right sides together.
- Stitch rows together with ¼" seams, aligning block intersections.
- Repeat, joining all rows to complete the design.

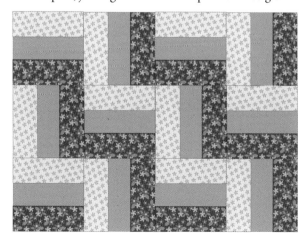

COLOR CONFIDENCE ▬

Coordinate or contrast Triple Rail colors to give your quilt personality. The dark fabrics create a dominant design. Sketch out your design before you start to quilt to eliminate surprises!

Select light, medium, and dark fabrics from color coordinates that are not in the same color family.

Piece together two groups of coordinating light, medium, and dark fabrics with the lightest color fabric used in both stratas.

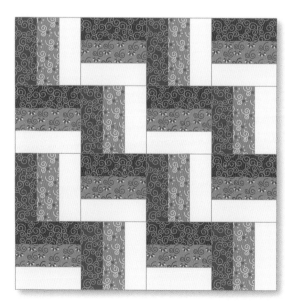

Roman Candle Block

The Roman Candle is very similar to the Triple Rail except it uses two stratas instead of one. See p. 36 for block size information.

Note: All seams are ¼" unless otherwise stated.

Select Fabrics

Choose three fabrics. Label them Fabric A, Fabric B, and Fabric C.

Cut Fabric into Strips

1 Cut three crosswise strips of Fabric A.

2 Cut one crosswise strip of Fabric B.

3 Cut two crosswise strips of Fabric C.

Stitch Strips into Strata

1 Form two groupings, each with three strips.
  - Strata 1: Position a Fabric B strip in the center of two Fabric A strips.
  - Strata 2: Position a Fabric A strip in the center of two Fabric C strips.

2 Prepare Strata 1.
  - Join strips A and B, right sides together.
  - Join the remaining strip A to the B strip, right sides together, to complete the first strata.
  - Press seams toward the darker fabric.

3 Prepare Strata 2 in the same way, joining strips as shown, right sides together.

Fabric A

Fabric B

Fabric A

Fabric C

Fabric A

Fabric C

Subcut Strata and Complete Blocks

1 Straighten the edge of each strata as detailed on p. 20, aligning the ruler's horizontal markings with the cut edge of the strips.

2 Cut blocks to finished size.

3 Arrange the blocks in two stacks, one for each strata.

4 Rotate Strata 2 sections 90° so they are perpendicular to Strata 1.

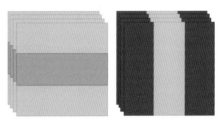

5 Join one of each strata, chain stitching them into pairs. Then clip the threads between pairs to separate them. Press seams flat, then to one side.

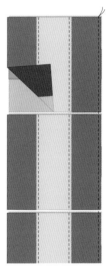

6 Arrange and join blocks.
  - Arrange blocks as desired.
  - Join blocks as detailed on p. 37, chain stitching when possible to save time and effort.
  - Join rows as detailed on p. 37 to complete the design.

COLOR CONFIDENCE

By changing the block arrangement and/or the color of the blocks you can create some very interesting designs. Experiment with designs. It's amazing how different the same blocks can look when you combine them in interesting ways.

Alternate 6" horizontal and vertical blocks to achieve these Roman Candle variations. The blocks are arranged the same, but the colors are different for a completely different feel.

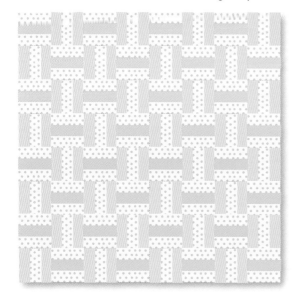 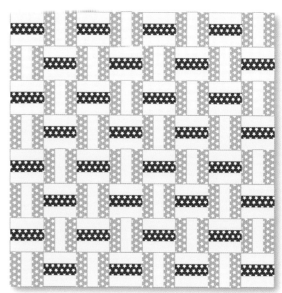

DESIGN DIVERSITY

Combine smaller blocks to form larger blocks; then add solid colored blocks for added interest.

Combine four 6" Roman Candle blocks (two strata) to form a 12" block, then alternate with two pieced and two solid 6" squares (with one strata the same as in the first block) to form a second 12" block.

Use nine 4" pieced blocks (two strata) to form 12" blocks; alternate those blocks with 12" blocks cut from two different solid colored fabrics.

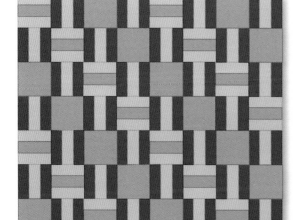 

chapter 3

Log Cabin Variations

Start with a center block and add strips or "logs" to create a novel quilted design. Use chain piecing to assemble the blocks—it's quick and easy. Vary colors, size, and piecing order for endless possibilities!

Framed Square

Add "logs" or strips to each side of a square to piece the Framed Square block. These blocks are easy enough for beginners, yet offer seasoned quilters many layout possibilities to challenge their imagination and skill.

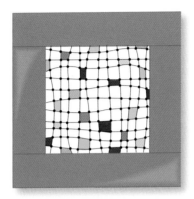

Create easy framed center blocks utilizing strata and chain piecing. It's more fun than framing a picture, and there are many more possibilities with fabric!

Select Fabrics

1 Select a solid or print (center square). Label it Fabric A.

2 Select two contrasting or coordinating fabrics (frames). Label them Fabrics B and C.

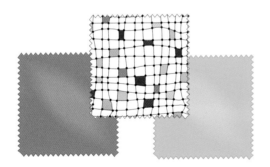

Block Size (Includes ¼" seam allowances on all edges.)
6½" finished block:
- 4½"-wide center strip
- 1½"-wide frame strips

Cut Fabric into Strips

1 Fabric A: Cut two 4½" strips.

2 Fabrics B and C: Cut four 1½" crosswise strips of each.

Stitch Strips into Strata

Note: All seams are ¼" unless otherwise stated.

1 Join strips together, forming a strata.
- Place one Fabric B strip over one Fabric A strip, right sides together. Stitch, joining lengthwise edges.
- Place a second Fabric B strip over the opposite edge of Fabric A, right sides together. Stitch, joining lengthwise edges, to complete the strata. Press seams toward the darker strips.
- Repeat process, creating a second strata using Fabrics A and C.

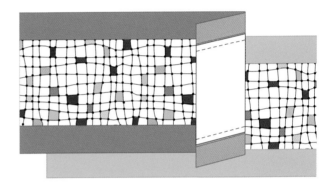

Subcut Strata and Complete Blocks

1 Straighten the edges of the stratas as detailed on p. 20, aligning the ruler's horizontal markings with the cut edge of the strips.

2 Subcut stratas into 4½" sections.

3 Add remaining Fabric B strips.
- Place one Fabric B strip on a work surface, right side up.
- Place 4½" Fabric A/B sections over the Fabric B strip, right sides together. The most recently pieced part of the section is at the top. Stitch, with lengthwise cut edges even.

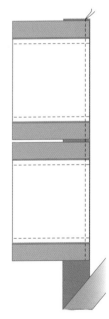

- Clip sections apart, press seams toward darker strips, and rotate sections 180°.
- Lay rotated section over remaining Fabric B strip, right sides together. Stitch, joining lengthwise edges, to complete the framed edge around the center block.

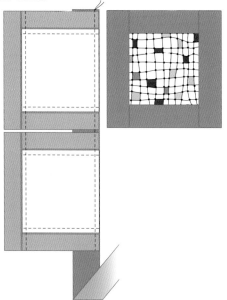

4 Repeat framing instructions using the second strata including Fabrics A and C, adding remaining Fabric C strips. Press seams toward the darker strips.

5 Separate and square blocks.

6 Stitch blocks together alternating light and dark frames for a quilt top.

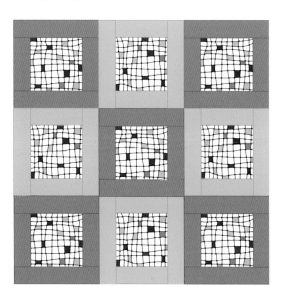

COLOR CONFIDENCE

Create a new look by advancing from all one-color centers to two colors, and then to all different centers, like scrappy or "I Spy" quilts.

Use only two fabrics, but reverse colorations in adjacent blocks. In one block, use Fabric A for the center and Fabric B for the frame strips. In the adjacent block, use Fabric B for the center and Fabric A for the frames.

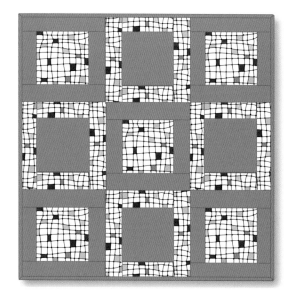

Alternate three colors for the frames, and a different 4½" square for each center of this "I Spy" quilt.

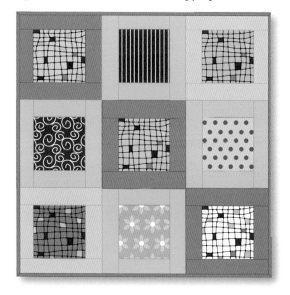

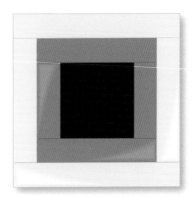

A favorite variation of the Framed Square block is referred to as Around the Hearth. It is put together basically the same as the Framed Square, except you add four or eight more logs to each block. Heartwarming!

Select Fabrics

1 Select a dark center square (often burgundy or deep red). Label it Fabric A.

2 Select a medium color for the middle logs (frames). Label them Fabric B.

3 Select a light color for the outer logs. Label them Fabric C.

Block Size (Includes ¼" seam allowances on all edges.)
12½" finished block:
- 4½"-wide center strip
- 2½"-wide frame strips

Cut Fabric into Strips
- Fabric A: Cut one 4½" strip.
- Fabrics B and C: Cut two 2½" strips of each.

Add Strips to Complete Blocks

Note: All seams are ¼" unless otherwise stated.

1 See instructions for Framed Square pp. 42–43, starting with Stitch Strips into Strata.

2 Repeat step three, adding Fabric C logs to all outer edges.

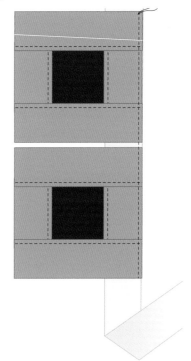

3 Press seams toward the darker strips.

4 Separate and square blocks.

5 Stitch blocks together for a quilt top, if desired.

COLOR CONFIDENCE

This simple Around the Hearth quilt becomes a show-stopper when colors are changed to fit the mood of the room in which it is showcased.

Alternate center block colors and first row of logs. Use the same color for the second row of logs.

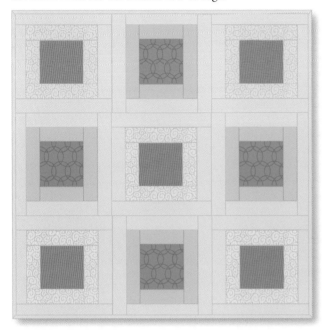

Use the same center block, and use scrappy options for the logs.

Reverse the light and dark colorations in alternating blocks for a contemporary version of Around the Hearth.

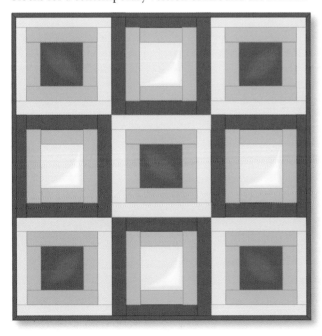

Reverse the colorations of the typical Around the Hearth blocks. Use light centers, medium first frames, and dark outside frames.

T-Shirt Square

This technique is perfect for T-shirt squares. Stitch a quilt for your favorite graduate using shirts with special memories, or use those T-shirts from your travels for a "Been There—Done That" quilt.

Select Fabrics

1 Select retired T-shirts (center squares), and a fusible knit interfacing backing.

2 Select contrasting or coordinating fabric (frames).

Block Size (Includes ¼" seam allowances on all edges.)
12½" finished block for T-shirt squares:
- 13"-wide interfaced T-shirt squares for each center block (trimmed to size after fusing)
- 2½"-wide frame strips

Cut Fabric

1 Cut out an approximately 13" square from the center front of the T-shirt.

2 Fuse knit interfacing the same size as the T-shirt fabric to the wrong side, centering interfacing over the back of the printed design.

3 Cut an 8½" square from the T-shirt.
- Use Omnigrid® Glow-Line™ Tape to mark an 8½" square on a large square ruler, such as the 12½" square Omnigrip™ Non-Slip Ruler. This provides a readily visible marking and cutting guide. Simply apply tape to the back of the ruler over the desired measurement. This tape peels off easily and leaves no sticky residue.

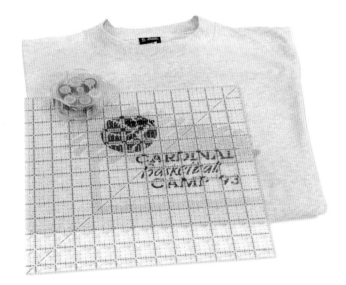

- Mark T-shirt with a water-soluble marking pen, centering the design. Be sure to remove these marks before pressing or they may be difficult to remove.
- Cut out the square with a rotary cutter.

4 Cut four 2½" crosswise frame strips from a second fabric.

Add Strips to Complete Blocks

Note: All seams are ¼" unless otherwise stated.

1 Lay one side of each center square over the first frame strip, right sides together, chain stitching squares to strip. Stitch and trim.

2 Lay the opposite side of the center square over the second frame strip, right sides together. Stitch and trim.

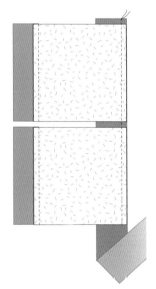

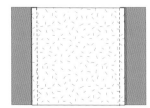

3 Press seams toward the darker strips.

4 Repeat, stitching the top and bottom of each square to the two remaining strips.

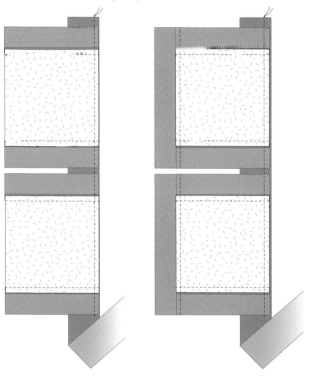

5 Press seams toward the darker strips.

6 Separate and square blocks.

7 Stitch blocks together for a quilt top, if desired.

Sew T-shirt blocks together or alternate them with print/solid fabric blocks or simple pieced blocks of the same size. Or, see pp. 86–89 for sashing and cornerstone ideas.

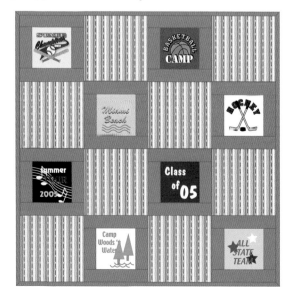

Creative Framed Square

2 Select contrasting or coordinating fabric (frames).

Turn a Creative Framed Square into a pillow, lap quilt, or table runner—just make the frame wider. Or, for another interesting variation, add a small embroidery to the center.

Select Fabrics

1 Select a fussy-cut print, embroidered design, or pre-printed design square (center square).

Block Size

Use a 6½" finished block (including ¼" seam allowances on all edges) for fussy-cut prints, embroidered designs, or preprinted design squares.

- 4½"-wide center squares for each block
- 1½"-wide frame strips

Cut Fabric

1 Cut 4½" squares fussy-cut prints, embroidered designs, or pre- printed design squares. The Get Squared™ Ruler Combo is the perfect tool for fussy cutting because you can audition designs using the 4½"-square center opening. Then cut with your rotary cutter. A unique teardrop design enables you to cut right to the corners.

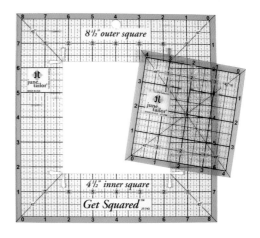

2 Cut 1½" crosswise strips from a second fabric (frames).

Add Strips to Complete Blocks

Join strips to squares and complete blocks for the project following instructions for T-shirt square on pp. 46–47.

Courthouse Steps

The Courthouse Steps are a continuation of the Framed Square (pp. 48–49). All of the dark fabrics are added to the middle, left, and right sides; all of the light fabrics are added to the top and bottom.

Note: All seams are ¼" unless otherwise stated.

Select Fabrics

1 Select one light and one dark fabric (frames and center).

2 Label one Fabric A, and the other, Fabric B.

Block Size (Includes ¼" seam allowances on all edges.)

12½" finished block:
- 4½"-wide center strip
- 2½"-wide frame strips

Cut Strips for Sample Blocks

1 Fabric A:
- Cut one 4½"-wide crosswise strip.
- Cut four 2½" crosswise strips.

2 Fabric B: Cut four 2½" crosswise strips.

Stitch Strips into Strata

1 Stitch strips together, forming a strata.
- Arrange one Fabric B strip over one 4½" Fabric A strip, right sides together.
- Stitch strips, joining lengthwise edges to form a strata. Rotate 180°.

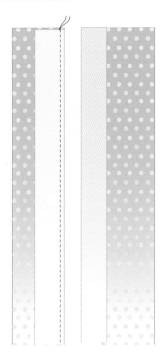

- Place a second Fabric B strip over the opposite side of the Fabric A strip, right sides together. Stitch, joining lengthwise edges to complete strata.

2 Press seams toward the outer strips.

Subcut Strata and Complete Blocks

1   Straighten the edge of each strata as detailed on p. 20, aligning the ruler's horizontal markings with the cut edge of the strips. Subcut 4½" sections. Stack sections.

2   Lay one 2½" Fabric A strip on a work surface, right side up.

3   Meet 8½" edges of a section to the Fabric A strip, right sides together. Stitch, with lengthwise raw edges even.

4   Continue to add sections to the strip and chain stitch sections together in the same manner. Separate sections.

5   Rotate sections 180°.

6   Lay the second Fabric A 2½" strip on a work surface, right side up.

7   Place the remaining 8½" edges of the sections over the Fabric A strip, right sides together. Stitch, with lengthwise raw edges even.

8   Press seams toward the outer strips.

9   Straighten the edge of each section as detailed on p. 20, aligning the ruler's horizontal markings with the cut edge of the section. Sections will be 8½" square.

10   Repeat process, adding two strips of Fabric B, and then two of Fabric A. Stitch, with lengthwise raw edges even, placing the most recently pieced part of the section at the top. Press seams toward the darker strips.

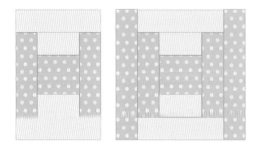

11   Separate and square blocks.

12   Stitch blocks together for a quilt top or table runner, if desired.

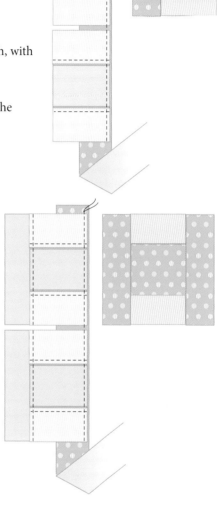

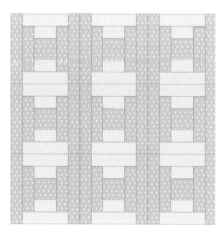

Courthouse Steps

COLOR CONFIDENCE

Alternate block colors, vary the color intensity, or choose several different solid colors for subtle but unique changes.

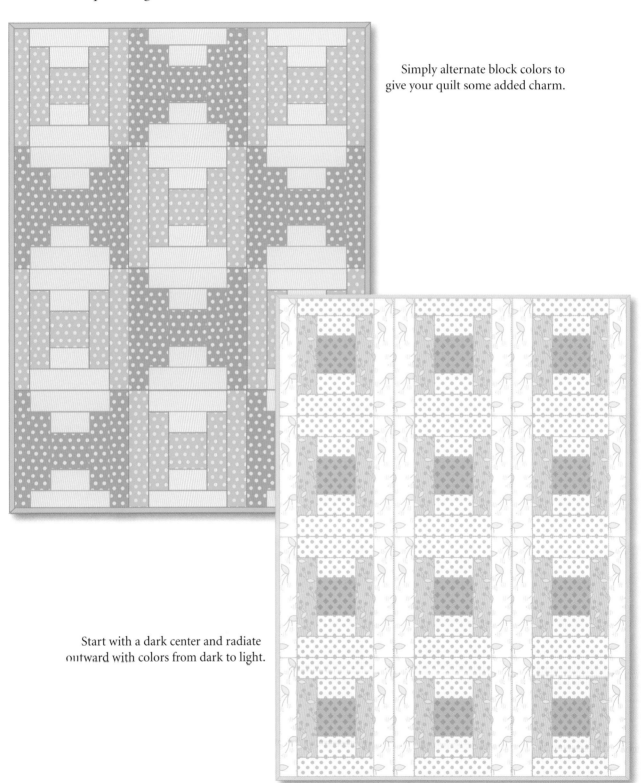

Simply alternate block colors to give your quilt some added charm.

Start with a dark center and radiate outward with colors from dark to light.

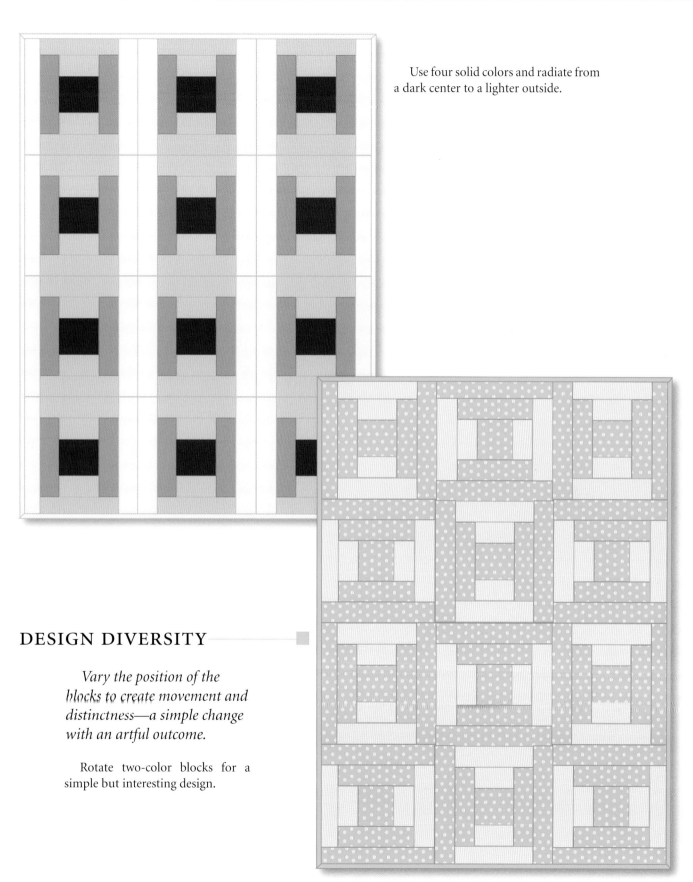

Use four solid colors and radiate from a dark center to a lighter outside.

DESIGN DIVERSITY

Vary the position of the blocks to create movement and distinctness—a simple change with an artful outcome.

Rotate two-color blocks for a simple but interesting design.

Simplified Log Cabin

A traditional Log Cabin block contains half light and half dark fabric, with 12 logs surrounding a center square.

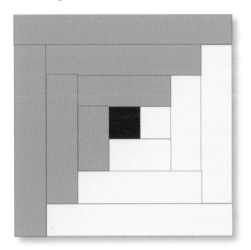

This easy version of the Log Cabin has fewer logs and it starts with a larger center block. It goes together quickly using the chain piecing method to stitch the logs around the center.

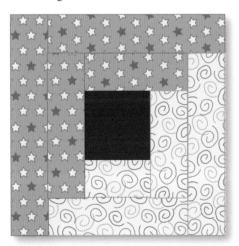

Select Fabrics

Select one dark Fabric A (center), one light Fabric B, and one medium Fabric C (logs). Label each accordingly.

Block Size (Includes ¼" seam allowances on all edges.)

12½" finished block:
- 4½"-wide dark center strip
- 2½"-wide log strips

Cut Fabric into Strips

1 Fabric A (dark): Cut one 4½"-wide center strip.

2 Fabric B (light): Cut four 2½"-wide log strips.

3 Fabric C (medium): Cut four 2½"-wide log strips.

Stitch Strips into Strata

1 Stitch strips together, forming a strata.
- Lay one 2½" Fabric B strip over one 4½" Fabric A strip, right sides together.
- Stitch, joining lengthwise edges to form a strata.

2 Press seam toward darker fabric.

Subcut Strata and Complete Blocks

1 Straighten the edge of the strata as detailed on p. 20, aligning the ruler's horizontal markings with the cut edge of the strips.

2 Subcut strata into 4½" sections.

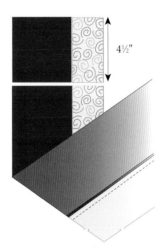

3 Lay second 2½" Fabric B strip on a work surface, right side up.

4 Place strata over the Fabric B strip, right sides together. The most recently pieced part of the section is at the top. Stitch, with lengthwise raw edges even.

5 Add additional strata sections, right sides together, chain stitching in the same manner. Press seams toward logs.

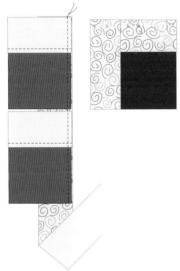

6 Trim edges of strip B even with strata.

7 Lay a 2½" Fabric C strip on a work surface, right side up.

8 Place the pieced section over the Fabric C strip, right sides together. The most recently pieced part of the section is at the top. Stitch, with lengthwise raw edges even.

9 Continue to "kiss" and add sections to the strip, chain stitching in the same manner. Press seams toward logs.

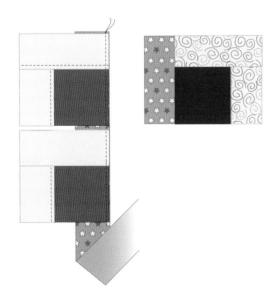

10 Lay another 2½" Fabric C strip on a work surface, right side up, and stitch, placing the most recently pieced part of the section at the top. Press.

11 Continue adding two additional Fabric B and two additional Fabric C strips to complete the block, always placing the most recently pieced part of the section at the top.

12 Stitch blocks together for a quilt top, if desired.

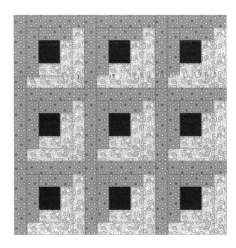

Simplified Log Cabin

COLOR CONFIDENCE

Change the color value of the center squares and logs to create a quilt that makes the design pop or becomes a subdued overall pattern. Chevrons and squares are created by the positioning of the dark and light logs.

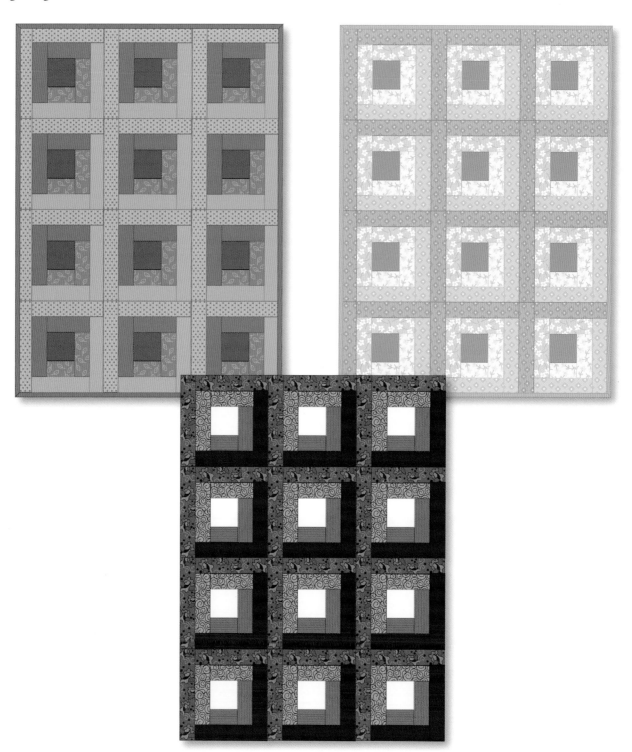

DESIGN CONFIDENCE

This simple block has many design possibilities. The use of color and the block arrangement are your designing tools. Create to your heart's content!

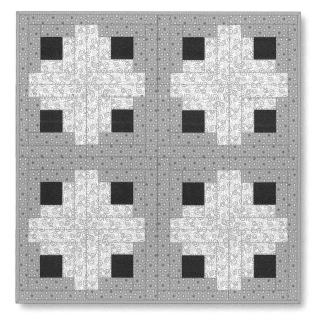

Place mirror imaged blocks next to each other.

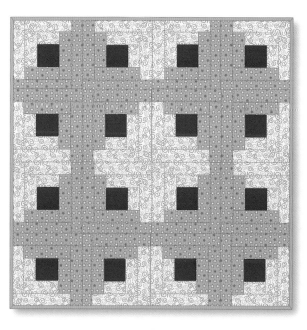

Rotate each block featured in quilt on left 180°.

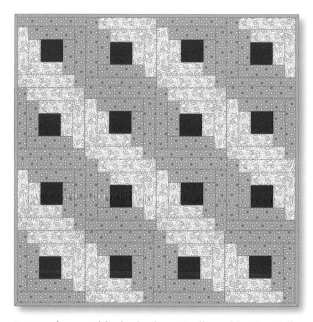

Rotate alternate blocks, both vertically and horizontally.

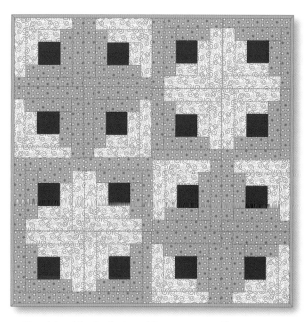

Combine blocks featured in top two quilts.

Uneven Log Cabin

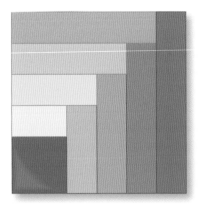

In an Uneven Log Cabin the first square is positioned in one corner rather than in the center of the block. Make this simple variation for 12½" finished blocks.

Select Fabrics

1 Choose one dark and one light fabric. Or, use five fabrics in gradation from medium to dark and four fabrics in gradation from light to medium.

2 Label the dark fabrics "A" and the light fabrics "B." If you are using colors that are in gradation from light to dark, label the darks 1A (Center), 3A, 5A, 7A, and 9A in the order they are placed. Label the lights that are in gradation 2B, 4B, 6B, and 8B. It doesn't matter if the gradation from the center is light to dark or dark to light. Just be consistent with your arrangement.

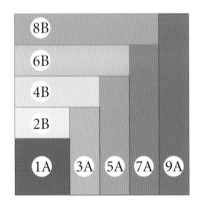

Block Size (Includes ¼" seam allowances on all edges.)
12½" finished blocks:
- 4½"-wide center strip
- 2½"-wide log strips

Cut Fabric into Strips

1 Fabric A (Use five fabrics ranging from medium to dark):
- Cut one 4½" strip (centers).
- Cut four 2½" strips in gradation from medium to dark.

2 Fabric B (Use four fabrics ranging from light to medium): Cut four 2½" strips in gradation from light to medium.

Stitch Strips into Strata

1 Stitch strips together, forming a strata.
- Place one 2½" Fabric 2B (light) strip over one 4½" Fabric 1A strip, right sides together.
- Stitch, joining lengthwise edges to form a strata.

2 Press seam toward Fabric 2B (log).

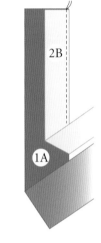

Subcut Strata and Complete Blocks

1 Straighten the edge of each strata as detailed on p. 20, aligning the ruler's horizontal markings with the cut edge of the strips.

2 Subcut strata into 4½" sections.

3 Place a 2½" Fabric 3A (medium) strip on a work surface, right side up.

4 Place a 4½" section over the Fabric 3A strip, right sides together. The most recently pieced part of the section is at the **bottom**. Stitch, with lengthwise edges even.

5 Continue to add sections to the strip and chain stitch in the same manner. Press seams toward log.

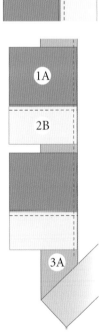

6 Trim edges of strip 3A even with sections.

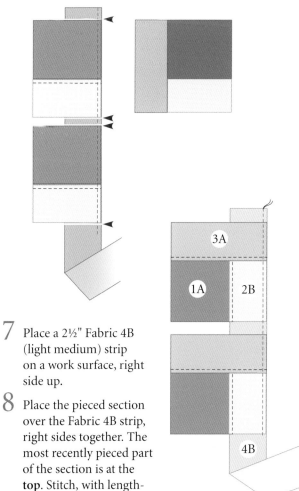

7 Place a 2½" Fabric 4B (light medium) strip on a work surface, right side up.

8 Place the pieced section over the Fabric 4B strip, right sides together. The most recently pieced part of the section is at the **top**. Stitch, with lengthwise edges even.

9 Continue to add sections to the strip and chain stitch in the same manner. Press seam toward log.

10 Trim edges of strip 4B even with sections.

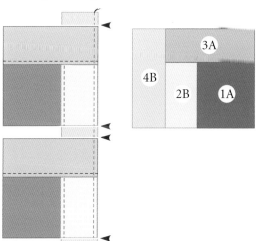

11 Place a 2½" strip of Fabric 5A on a work surface, right side up. Stitch sections to the strip, with the most recently pieced part at the **bottom**. Press.

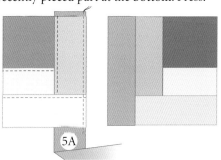

12 Trim edges of strip 5A even with sections.

13 Continue adding two additional light to medium strips on one side and medium to dark strips on the other side to complete the blocks. See order as illustrated.

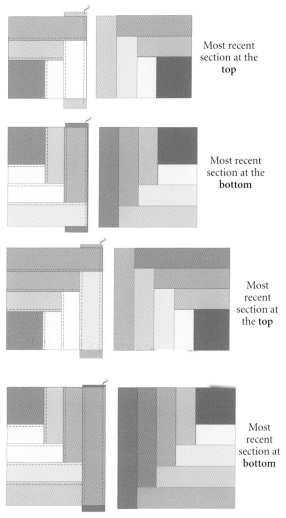

Most recent section at the **top**

Most recent section at the **bottom**

Most recent section at the **top**

Most recent section at **bottom**

Rotate block to duplicate that shown at upper left on p. 58. Join multiple blocks to make a quilt top, if desired.

Uneven Log Cabin

COLOR CONFIDENCE

Play with the value and intensity of the colors used in a quilt to emphasize different areas of the design, as well as create vertical or horizontal movement.

DESIGN DIVERSITY

Create depth and excitement by the diverse arrangements.

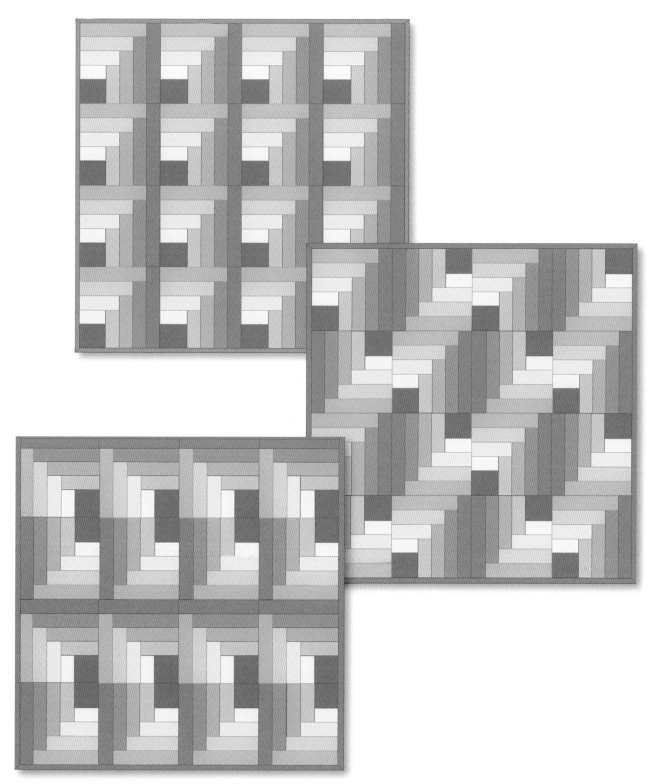

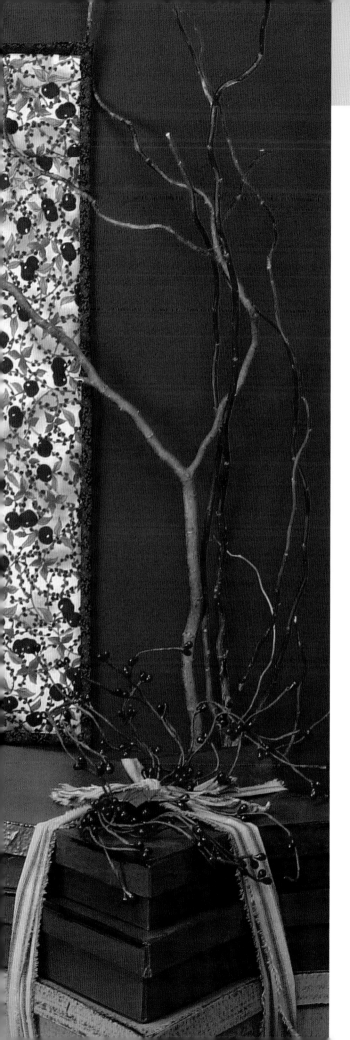

chapter 4

Squares and Triangles

Achieve the look of triangles—
without cutting a single one!
Our adaptation features the use of
squares to create triangles. Combine
half-square or quarter-square
triangles into blocks with easy
creative options.

Wall hanging by Karen Zilke
For instructions, see pp. 120–123.

Half-Square Triangles

Amazingly enough, the blocks in this chapter all start with squares, and many of the squares have become triangles! You can easily create the blocks with a combination of squares, rectangles, half-square triangles, and quarter-square triangles.

The traditional way of making half- and quarter-square triangles is to cut out triangles and sew them together to form squares. With our easy method, the squares are sewn first—then cut. Chain piecing completes projects quickly!

Make half-square triangles by taking two fabric squares, sewing diagonally with right sides together, then cutting the squares in half diagonally between stitching lines. Voila—two half-square triangles!

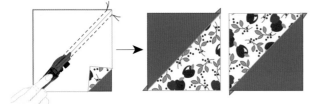

Select Fabrics

1 Select two contrasting fabrics.

2 Use both fabrics for each block.

Block Size (Includes ¼" seam allowances on all edges.)
- 3½" block: Cut 3⅞" squares.
- 4½" block: Cut 4⅞" squares.
- 6½" block: Cut 6⅞" squares.

Cut Fabrics

Note: The following instructions reference making a 6½" finished square. Adjust square sizes as listed at below left to make other sizes.

1 Light fabric: Cut one 6⅞" square.

2 Dark fabric: Cut one 6⅞" square.

> ### NOTE FROM NANCY
> *Omnigrid® Glow-Line™ Tape is a great aid when cutting odd sized squares. Simply apply the tape to the back of a square ruler at the desired measurement and cut out the square with a rotary cutter. See additional Glow-Line Tape information on p. 46.*

Complete Half-square Triangles

1 Place light and dark 6⅞" squares right sides together.

2 Mark a diagonal line from one corner to the opposite corner, and mark ¼" seam allowances on each side of the diagonal line.

> ### NOTE FROM NANCY
> *Use the Quick Quarter for ease in marking half-square triangles. The center slot provides an accurate line for marking the diagonal line, and edges provide a perfect ¼" seam allowance on both sides.*

3 Stitch on each of the marked seam allowance lines.

4 Cut the squares apart on the diagonal line between seam allowances.

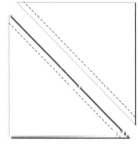

5 Press seam allowances toward the darker fabric.

6 Whenever you use multiple half-square triangles to create a design, chain piece them together to simplify construction.
- Arrange the squares according to your design.
- Meet right sides of two squares for the first row. Stitch seam.
- "Kiss" the pair of squares for the second row to the first squares; continue stitching.

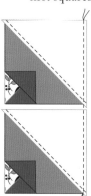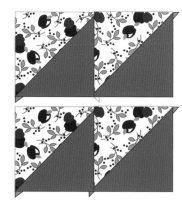

- Clip threads to separate squares. Press seams flat, then to one side.

■ NOTE FROM NANCY
Press seams in adjacent rows in opposite directions to make it easier to align seam intersections.

- Join rows, matching seam intersections.

7 When the design includes more than two squares in a row:
- Chain stitch the first two squares in each row together, as detailed above.
- Repeat for second set of squares. Clip threads to separate pairs. Press seams flat, then to one side, pressing seams in adjacent rows in opposite directions.

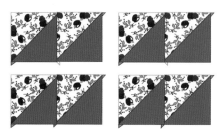

- Stitch the pairs together to form horizontal rows. Press seams in adjacent rows in opposite directions.

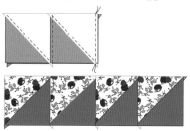

- Stitch horizontal rows together, matching seam intersections.

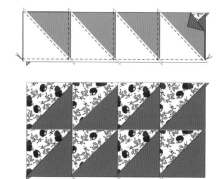

- If there are three squares in a row, chain the pairs together as before. Then chain the remaining squares to each row before stitching the horizontal rows together.

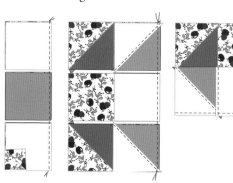

■ NOTE FROM NANCY
Instead of combining only half-square triangles, include solid blocks to obtain a design such as the one shown at right.

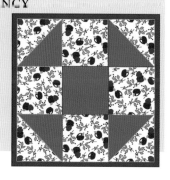

Windmill

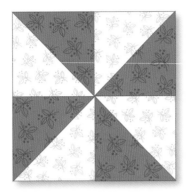

Make a large Windmill block for a pillow or combine it with other blocks for a quilt or table runner. This versatile block is fun to make and has a myriad of uses.

1 Cut fabrics.
- Light fabric: Cut two 6⅞" squares.
- Dark fabric: Cut two 6⅞" squares.

2 Follow instructions on p. 64 to make four half-square triangle blocks. Arrange blocks following illustration for placement.

3 Join squares for each row following instructions on p. 65. Press seams of adjacent rows in opposite directions. Then join rows, aligning seam intersections. Press.

4 If desired, make additional blocks, cutting additional squares and chain piecing pairs together. Alternate them with solid colored blocks of the same size if desired.

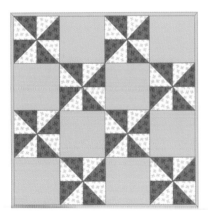

COLOR CONFIDENCE

Use four unique dark prints in the same color family with four coordinating light fabrics for a scrappy windmill variation. Combine windmills with solid colored blocks if desired.

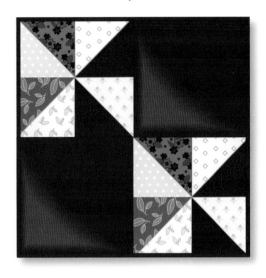

DESIGN DIVERSITY

Combine the windmill blocks with smaller blocks to add some pizzazz. Make the smaller windmill blocks using 3⅞" squares for the half-square triangles. Combine smaller windmill blocks with solid 6½" blocks to create 12½" finished blocks. Then alternate large and smaller combination blocks.

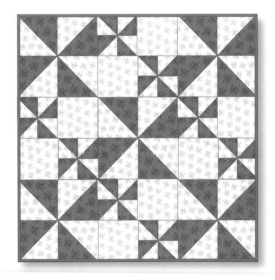

Flying Geese

Flying Geese blocks give direction to quilted projects! They force your eyes to follow the design. A smaller version of Flying Geese blocks is a wonderful addition to borders and sashing.

1 Cut fabrics.
   • Light fabric: Cut two 6⅞" squares.
   • Dark fabric: Cut two 6⅞" squares.

2 Follow instructions on p. 64 to make four half-square triangle blocks.

3 Join two half-square triangle blocks for each row, following illustration for placement. Stitch, positioning dark fabrics right sides together. Press seams in adjacent rows in opposite directions.

4 Join rows following instructions on p. 65.

5 If desired, make additional blocks and rows following the same procedure, stitching additional half-square triangles and chain piecing pairs together before joining rows.

COLOR CONFIDENCE

Alternating colors in each row creates horizontal lines within the quilt.

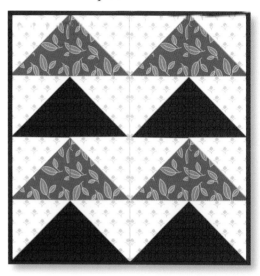

DESIGN DIVERSITY

Vary the size of the Flying Geese blocks for a totally new look.

Alternate solid blocks with Hour Glass blocks to create a wealth of design possibilities. Hour Glass blocks are often set in diagonal rows "on point," as the design blends well with setting and corner triangles. (See pp. 84–85.)

1 Cut fabric. Use two squares and two half-square triangles for each block.
   • Light Fabric A: Cut one 6⅞" square.
   • Dark Fabric B: Cut one 6⅞" square.
   • Print Fabric C: Cut two 6½" squares.

2 Prepare half-square triangles as detailed on p. 64. Arrange squares and half-square triangles to form rows, following illustration for placement.

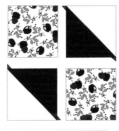

3 Join rows following instructions on p. 65 to complete the blocks.

4 If desired, make additional blocks following the same procedure.

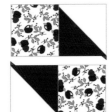

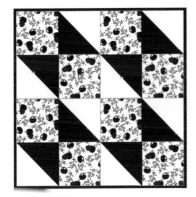

DESIGN DIVERSITY

Isn't it amazing how rotating every other block 90° changes the entire design to one that looks like a planned star?

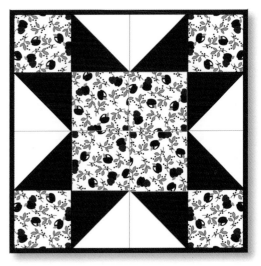

COLOR AND DESIGN CONFIDENCE

Caution—value at work! Change designs by merely changing the value from light to medium or dark.

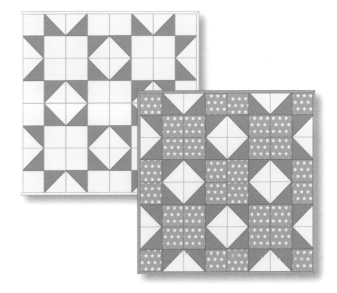

Friendship Star

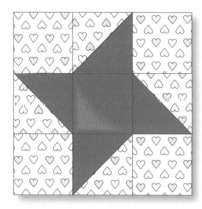

The 12½" half-square triangle blocks shared on the next few pages all start with 4½" squares. Try one of the following variations or create your own blocks.

1 Cut fabrics for each block.
- Light Fabric A:
  - Cut two 4⅞" squares for making half-square triangle blocks.
  - Cut four 4½" squares.
- Dark Fabric B:
  - Cut two 4⅞" squares for making half-square triangle blocks.
  - Cut one 4½" square.

2 Prepare four half-square triangle blocks from 4⅞" squares following general instructions on p. 64.

3 Arrange squares and half-square triangle blocks to form rows, following illustration below for placement and directions for three squares in a row on p. 65. Stitch. Press seams in adjacent rows in opposite directions.

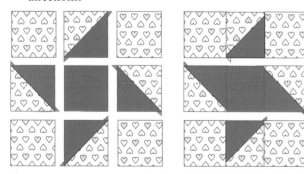

4 Join rows, right sides together.
- Join rows 1 and 2, right sides together, matching seam intersections.
- Join row 3 to row 2 to complete the block as shown above. Press seams.

COLOR AND DESIGN CONFIDENCE

Change the fabric colors to give the stars a totally different look.

Give this combination a serene updated look by changing the background colors.

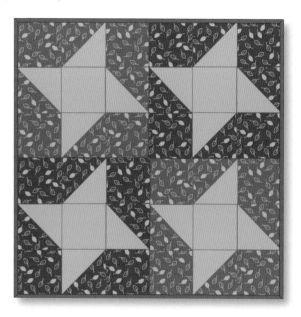

Use a light fabric for the star points to lift them and create movement.

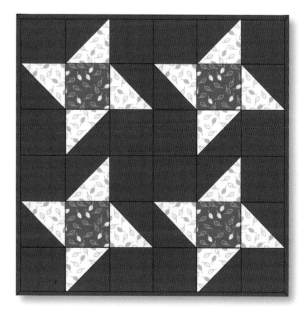

Shoo Fly

This variation uses the same amounts of light and dark fabrics for squares and half-square triangle blocks as the Friendship Star (p. 69). Layout is the only thing that changes. Use larger squares to make a pillow block, or place solid blocks alternately with the Shoo Fly blocks for a quilt.

1 Cut fabrics.
- Light Fabric A:
  - Cut two 4⅞" squares for making half-square triangle blocks.
  - Cut four 4½" squares.
- Dark Fabric B:
  - Cut two 4⅞" squares for making half-square triangle blocks.
  - Cut one 4½" square.

2 Prepare four half-square triangle blocks from 4⅞" squares following general instructions on p. 64. Arrange squares and half-square triangle blocks to form rows, following illustration below for placement and directions for three squares in a row on p. 65. Stitch. Press seams in adjacent rows in opposite directions.

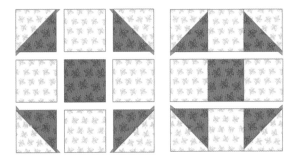

3 Join rows, right sides together.
- Join rows 1 and 2, matching seam intersections.
- Join row 3 to row 2 to complete the block as shown above. Press seams.

COLOR CONFIDENCE

A simple thing like a color change can create a totally different look. Have fun experimenting with different colorations.

Swap lights and darks to create interest. The center block appears to be set at an angle, but is really created by meeting dark corners in the center.

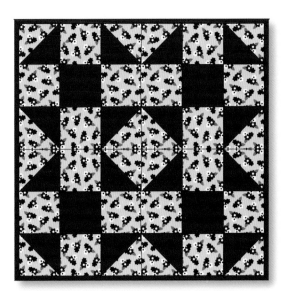

Introduce two new colors to the original block. The center block is a new dark color, and the other solid blocks are a new light color.

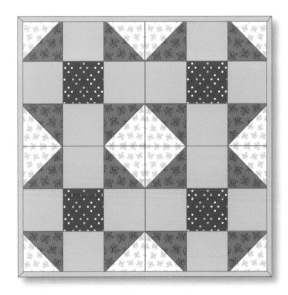

Churn Dash

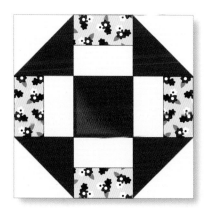

Create an interesting three color Churn Dash block incorporating half-square triangles, a solid square, and double rail squares. It's unique, and much easier than it looks!

1 Cut fabrics for each block.
- Light Fabric A:
  - Cut one 2½" crosswise strip for rectangle blocks.
  - Cut two 4⅞" squares for half-square triangle blocks.
- Dark Fabric B:
  - Cut one 4½" square for center block.
  - Cut two 4⅞" squares for half-square triangle blocks.
- Print Fabric C: Cut one 2½" crosswise strip for rectangle blocks.

2 Prepare four half-square triangle blocks from 4⅞" squares following general instructions on p. 64.

3 Prepare strata blocks.
- Form a strata by joining lengthwise edges of 2½" Fabric A and Fabric C strips. Press seam toward Fabric C.
- Subcut four 4½" blocks.

4 Arrange rectangle blocks, center square, and half-square triangle blocks to form rows, following illustration for placement. Stitch following directions for three squares in a row on p. 65. Press seams in adjacent rows in opposite directions.

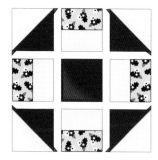 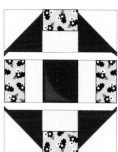

5 Join rows, right sides together.
- Join rows 1 and 2, matching seam intersections. Press.
- Join row 3 to complete block as shown above. Press.

COLOR AND DESIGN CONFIDENCE

Change fabric values in some or all of the fabrics for interesting color variations.

Change the center from a dark to a medium value and frame with darker strips.

Turn the original design topsy turvy! Use only two fabrics; change the values of corner blocks and rectangles.

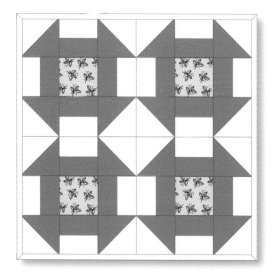 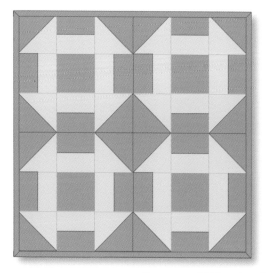

Quarter-Square Triangles

Make quarter-square triangles by taking two half-square triangle blocks, joining them right sides together, and cutting them in half diagonally between stitching lines.

Select Fabrics

Select two contrasting fabrics, one dark and one light, for each square. Fabrics may vary, depending on the combination desired for the quarter-square triangles.

Block Size: (Includes ¼" seam allowances on all edges.)

12½" finished block:
- 4½" block: Cut 5¼" squares.
- 6½" block: Cut 7¼" squares.

Cut Fabric

1 Light fabric: Cut one square of desired size, above.

2 Dark fabric: Cut one square of desired size.

Complete Quarter-square Triangles

1 Use one dark and one light square to make two half-square triangles following instructions on p. 64.

2 Join the half-square triangle blocks to make quarter-squares.
- Meet two half-square triangle blocks, right sides together, following illustration for placement. (Meet opposite colors on the two blocks.)

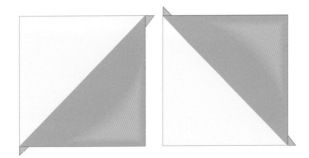

- Mark a diagonal line from one corner to the opposite corner, and mark ¼" seam allowances on each side of the diagonal line. Use a Quick Quarter, if desired; see p. 64.

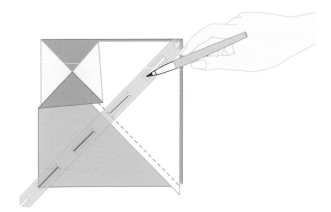

- Stitch on each of the marked seam allowance lines.

- Cut the squares apart on the diagonal line between seam allowances, forming two quarter-square triangle blocks.

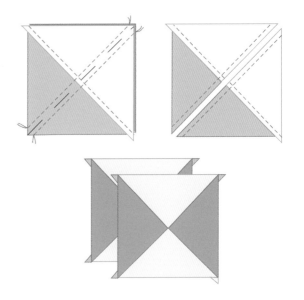

- Press seam allowances to one side.

3 Whenever you combine multiple solid and half- or quarter-square triangles to create a design, chain piece them together to simplify construction. See p. 65.

Ohio Star

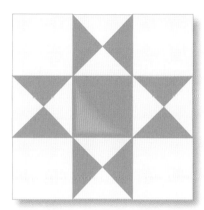

This versatile star block is quite popular and easy to piece. It is constructed with nine squares, using a combination of quarter-square triangles and solid squares.

1 Cut fabrics for each block.
  • Light Fabric A:
    - Cut four 4½" squares (outer squares).
    - Cut two 5¼" squares (quarter-square triangles).
  • Dark Fabric B:
    - Cut one 4½" square (center).
    - Cut two 5¼" squares (quarter-square triangles).

2 Prepare half-square triangles from light and dark 5¼" squares following instructions on p. 64.

3 Prepare quarter-square triangles from half-square triangle squares following instructions on p. 72.

4 Join quarter-square triangle squares and solid squares, right sides together, to form rows following placement illustration. Press seams in adjacent rows in opposite directions.

5 Join rows, right sides together, to form a block.

6 If desired, make additional blocks following the same procedure, cutting additional squares and chain piecing rows together.

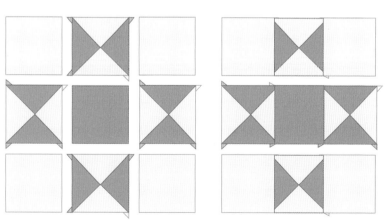

Ohio Star

COLOR AND DESIGN CONFIDENCE

Try these two- and three-fabric Ohio Star block variations. Each is easy, and yet creative!

Use two fabrics in this variation, using the light fabric for the solid blocks as well as in the quarter-square triangles.

Use three fabrics in this variation, with the center featuring a coordinating print.

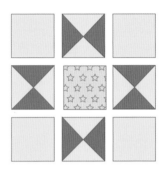

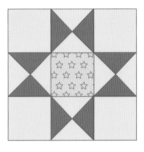

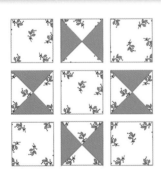

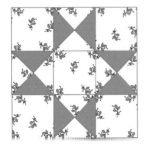

The entire star is one color in this easy variation that uses only two fabrics.

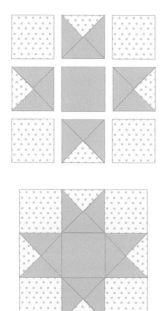

Three fabrics make up these blocks. The quarter-squares use three colors, with the third color placed next to the center square.

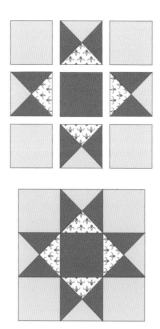

Snowball

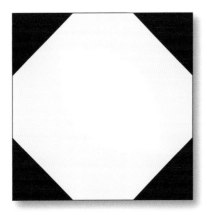

This timeless traditional block can be used as a single block in different colorations. Alternate it with solid squares to show off embroidery or quilting skills. Use it as a border treatment, or combine with nine-patch blocks for a spectacular quilt with visual movement, as shown on p. 82.

Basic Block Size (Includes ¼" seam allowances.)
- 6½" block = 2½" corner squares
- 12½" block = 4½" corner squares

Feel free to adjust corner squares to any size you prefer. Our illustration shows five different sized corners. Notice how smaller corner blocks make snowballs appear rounder.

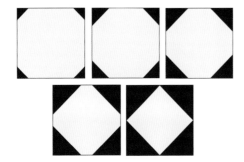

Cut Fabrics (Instructions make a 12½" finished block.)
- Light Fabric A: Cut one 12½" block.
- Dark Fabric B: Cut four 4½" squares.

Complete Snowball Block

1 Prepare corner squares.
- On wrong side of 4½" squares mark a solid diagonal line from corner to corner. Mark ½" away from the line as shown.

- Place the squares in each corner of the 12½" light square, right sides together.

2 Join the corner squares to the block.
- Stitch along the two marked stitching lines for each corner.

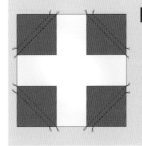

- Trim the corners between the stitching lines. Press seams toward darker corner fabrics. Save the remaining smaller half-square triangle blocks to use for a future project.

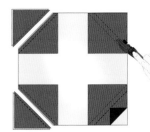

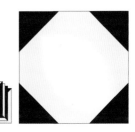

COLOR AND DESIGN CONFIDENCE

Once you know the technique for a basic Snowball block you can get creative! Use just about any size block for the corners, vary colors, or add an embroidery design to the center for fantastic variations.

Add embroidery to alternating light center squares. Use four different colorations for blocks, featuring two of the same color in each vertical row.

The color and stitching really pop in this combination! Use a different color for each corner and alternate the center quilting designs that are featured on the light blocks.

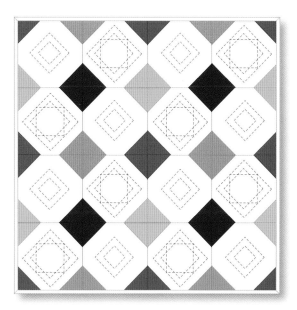

Use three different base fabrics and add corner squares that are all the same color. The lighter Snowballs rise to the surface!

Repeat the same block with a dark base with light corner blocks. The base blocks connect with an almost cutwork appearance!

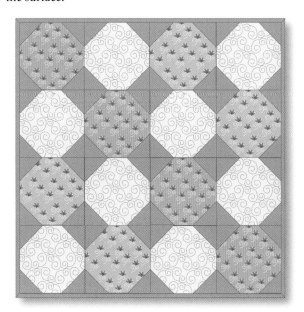

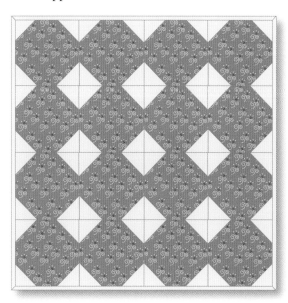

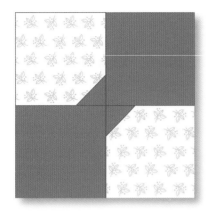

You learned to add corner squares while making the Snowball block—here's another variation using two different fabrics. Use one dark corner square on each of the two light squares, and add two dark squares to complete the block.

Block Size (Includes ¼" seam allowances on all edges.)
- 3½" blocks = 3½" squares, 1½" corner squares
- 6½" blocks = 6½" squares, 2½" corner squares

Cut Fabrics

(Instructions reference a 12½" finished block, with ¼" seam allowances on all edges.)
- Light Fabric A: Cut two 6½" squares.
- Dark fabric:
  - Cut two 6½" squares.
  - Cut two 2½" corner squares.

Complete Bow Tie Block

1 Prepare corner squares.
- On wrong side of 2½" corner squares mark a solid diagonal line from corner to corner. Mark ½" away from the first line as shown.

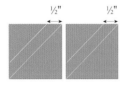

- Place a corner square in one corner of each 6½" light square, right sides together. Stitch along marked lines.

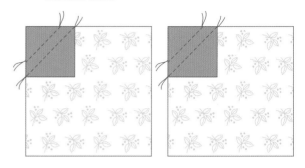

2 Join the corner squares to the blocks.
- Stitch along the two marked stitching lines on each corner square.
- Trim the corners, cutting between the stitching lines. Press seams toward darker corner fabrics. Save the remaining smaller blocks to use for a future project.

3 Join squares as illustrated, pressing seams in adjacent rows in opposite directions.

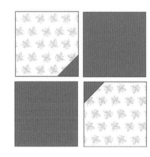 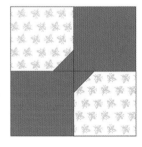

DESIGN DIVERSITY

Change the bow tie angle to create different designs for your quilt.

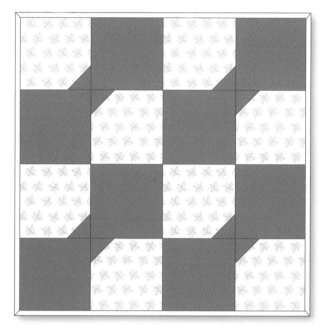

All blocks in each row angle in the same direction.

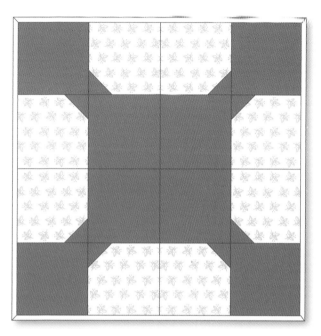

Alternate blocks, with dark squares in corners.

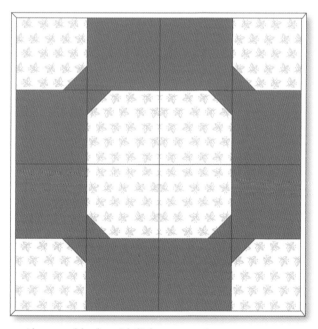

Alternate blocks with light squares in corners.

chapter 5

Combining Elements

Make a quilt that's "just the right size," or one that's the perfect artistic combination, by the positioning of the blocks and the addition of sashing, cornerstones, and borders.

Setting Blocks

Are you ready? Now that you've made some blocks, it's time to join them to make a project. The way in which blocks are positioned is referred to as "setting." Setting blocks side by side is a way to begin; it's so easy! Setting blocks on point is a bit more challenging, but opens up a wealth of interesting design possibilities.

Side by Side (Straight) Settings

A simple side by side setting is the most common way to set quilt blocks, especially for blocks that form secondary designs when sewn together. In a side by side setting the sides of the blocks run parallel to the sides of the quilt.

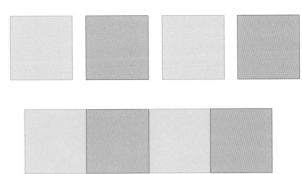

The following two straight set blocks include several sizes of 9-patch blocks, with Snowball blocks used as setting squares. In the second version, notice how the lighter colored squares, which are the same color as the Snowball blocks, stand out and form a secondary design.

The third example of a straight setting combines 12" Hour Glass stars and Snowball blocks. The design elements in these blocks form a secondary design as well.

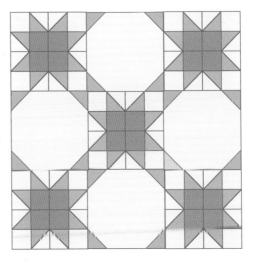

COLOR CONFIDENCE

Color has a big impact on every aspect of quilting. Shown below are straight set Snowball blocks. The first version includes light Snowballs with dark corners, whereas the second version alternates light Snowballs with dark corners and dark Snowballs with dark corners. The difference in value clearly makes the light Snowballs look as if they are floating on air.

Light Snowballs with dark corners

Light Snowballs with dark corners alternating with dark Snowballs with dark corners

"On Point" Settings

"On point" settings are sewn in diagonal rows, beginning in a corner, usually the top left corner. Use the same block throughout, or add solid blocks as setting squares. Quilt blocks set on point cover a larger area, so this is one way to increase the size of your quilt without having to piece additional blocks. The sides of the blocks run diagonally, at a 45° angle to the sides of the quilt. To create a rectangular or square design, you need to add setting triangles and corner triangles. Although those triangles sometimes intimidate a quilter because they look as if they are set in, adding them is really very simple. The secret: They are sewn on as the rows of blocks are stitched together, before rows are joined.

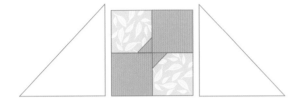
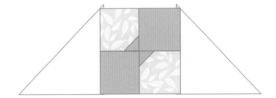

Setting Bow Tie Blocks On Point

Complete several Bow Tie blocks and use them to test your skill with an on point setting.

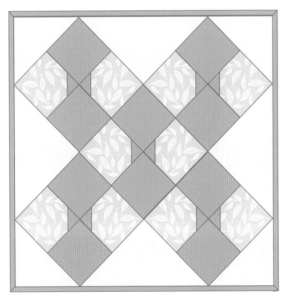

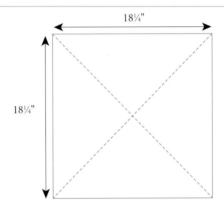

18¼"

18¼"

1 Create five 12½" Bow Tie blocks following instructions on p. 78.

2 Cut setting triangles.
   • Cut one 18¼" square.
   • Subcut into four setting triangles.
     - Cut diagonally from corner to corner as shown.
     - When adding the triangles to the design, place the base of the triangles (the longest side) on the outer edge of the project so that edge will be on the straight of grain.

Note from Nancy
Please keep in mind that bias edges of triangles should never be placed on the outside edge of a quilt.

3 Cut corner triangles.
   • Cut two 9⅜" squares; subcut each square into two triangles.
   • Cut diagonally from one corner to the other as shown. The base of the triangles (longest edge) is cut on the **bias** rather than on the straight of grain as with the setting triangles.

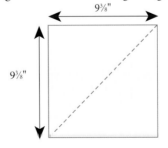

9⅜"

9⅜"

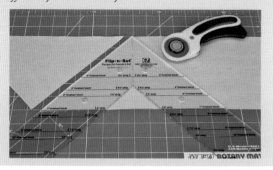
Here's a brief description of how to use the Flip•n•Set™ Tool:

- Open the Flip•n•Set™ Tool and locate the finished block size. Next to this measurement, you'll find the strip width needed for cutting the setting triangles.
- Cut strips that width.
- Lay the tool on the strip. Align the point at the top of the strip and the finished block measurement along the bottom of the strip. Cut along outer edges.

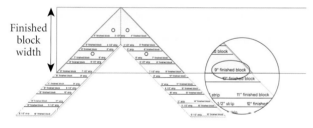

- Invert the tool, aligning its point with the bottom of the strip and its edge with the first cut edge. Cut a second triangle.

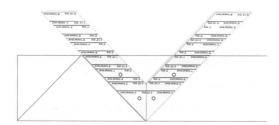

- Repeat, inverting the tool each time to cut the number of setting triangles needed.
- Cut two extra setting triangles, then cut them in half to provide the four corner triangles.

4 Lay out the quilt blocks and triangles in the way that they will be sewn.

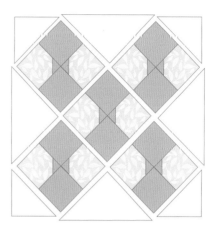

5 Stitch the blocks in each row together as shown. Press seams in adjacent rows in opposite directions.

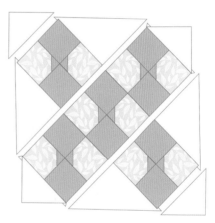

6 Sew rows together, adding the final two corner triangles to complete the project. Press seams to one side.

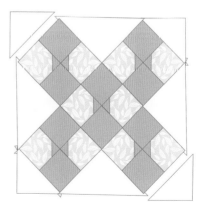

Simple Sashing

Sashing is the fabric strips, plain or pieced, that frame and separate quilt blocks. Sashing not only makes your quilt larger, but also draws design elements together for a total appeal. Match or contrast sashing to the quilt. Contrasting sashing defines the blocks and makes them stand out, while matching sashing blends in and becomes part of the block.

Add Sashing Pieces

1 Arrange blocks in the order that they will be sewn together.

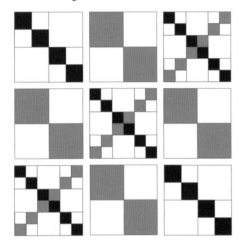

2 Add sashing to blocks in each row.
- Chain stitch the blocks to the sashing strip, right sides together, stitching sashing to the left side of each block.
- Cut blocks apart. Stitch another sashing strip to the right side of the last block in each row.
- Join sashed blocks in each row.

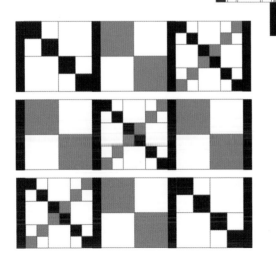

3 Add sashing between rows.
- Measure the length of the seamed rows. Cut sashing strips equal to that length.
- Stitch sashing to bottom of each row, plus on top of the first row.

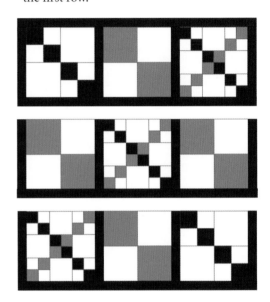

- Complete sashing by stitching the middle row to the top and bottom rows.

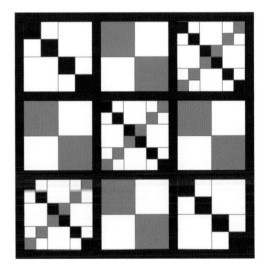

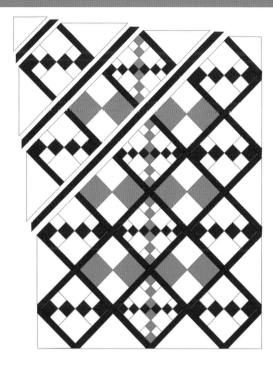

█ NOTE FROM NANCY

Diagonal set sashing also uses the same technique. The main difference is that rows of the blocks are positioned together diagonally, and setting and corner triangles are added.

DESIGN DIVERSITY ───█

Change the look of your quilt by changing the sashing. Narrow or wide, matching or contrasting—create a unique look that is perfect for your quilt!

Narrow sashing

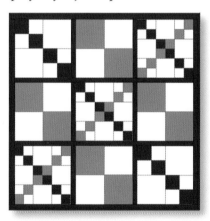

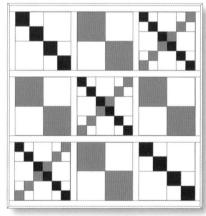

Matching sashing

Wide sashing

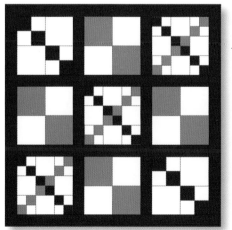

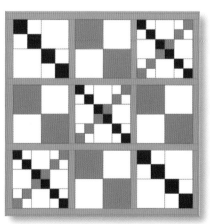

Contrasting sashing

Cornerstones

Cornerstones are square fabric blocks that connect two pieces of sashing or border strips at the corners. Using cornerstones is an alternative to having the sashing or borders "kiss", or miter, together. Add cornerstones to a quilt to give the design interest and artistic appeal. Cornerstones can also bring a design together and force your eyes to move across the quilt's surface.

Cornerstones can be as simple as solid colored blocks, an easy pieced block for the corner, an appliquéd block, or a pieced block with pieced sashing to create a secondary design. You've spent a lot of time creating the inside blocks so it is only fitting that the borders use design elements that relate to the blocks and enhance the beauty of the quilt.

DESIGN DIVERSITY

Use simple blocks and add decorative cornerstones to borders to enhance your quilt. For another option, add cornerstones to the sashing. Get creative!

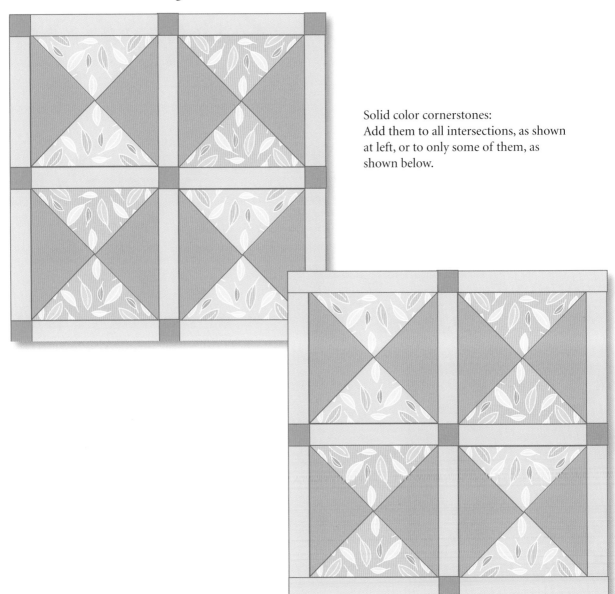

Solid color cornerstones:
Add them to all intersections, as shown at left, or to only some of them, as shown below.

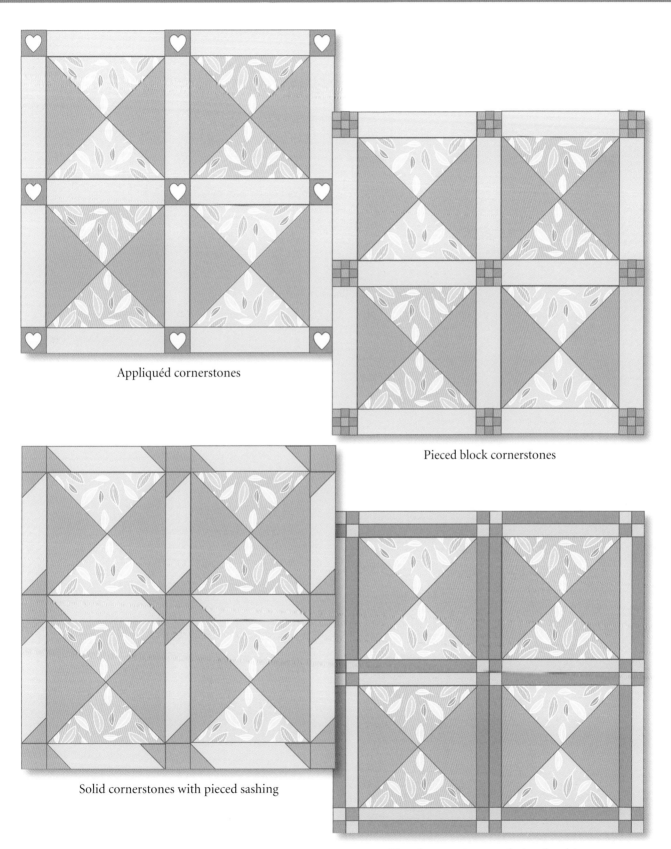

Appliquéd cornerstones

Pieced block cornerstones

Solid cornerstones with pieced sashing

Pieced cornerstones and pieced sashing

Borders

Add borders to a quilt setting to enhance the beauty and enlarge the quilt area without making additional blocks. Use one of the colors from within the quilt blocks for the border to intensify that color in the overall color scheme of the quilt, or use a coordinating color to add a little pizzazz.

1 Choose a border type:

- **Straight borders** are generally one piece of fabric on each edge of the quilt, but may be seamed on larger quilts.

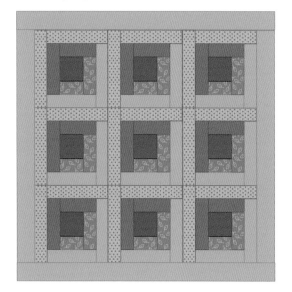

- **Pieced borders** can be a combination of various smaller blocks arranged to form a secondary design.

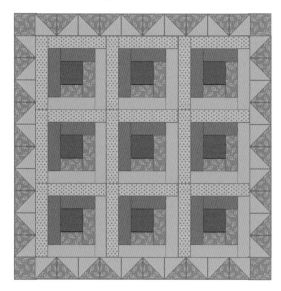

- **Scrappy borders** are a good way to give your quilt some color. Piece together strips of the same fabrics from the quilt top or include some that are totally different. Then attach the scrappy borders to your quilt.

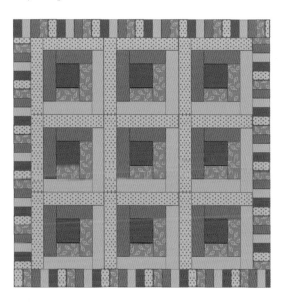

- **Mitered borders** are often used when you have multiple borders, or when it enhances the overall appearance of the quilt top. See pp. 92–93 for instructions for making mitered borders.

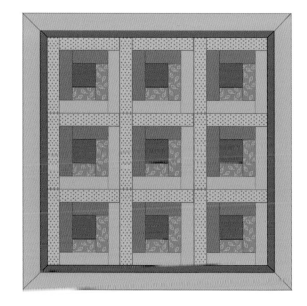

2 Measure the quilt and cut border lengths.

- Measure the center of the quilt top to bottom and side to side to determine the lengths of the border strips. It is important to use a center measurement rather than an end measurement to obtain an even quilt top.

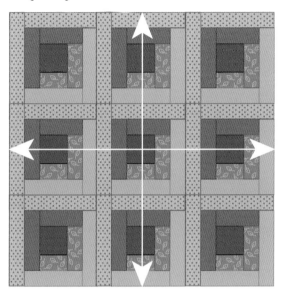

- Cut fabric on crosswise grain for border strips.
  - Cut side border strips as long as the center quilt measurement from top to bottom.
  - Cut top and bottom borders the length of the center quilt measurement from left to right, plus the width of the side border strips.
  - Diagonally piece strips that need to be longer than 42". Trim seams; then press seams open to reduce bulk.

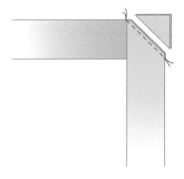

3 Stitch borders to the quilt.

- Stitch borders to the left and right edges of the quilt.

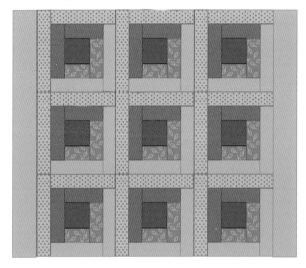

- Stitch borders to the top and bottom of the quilt.

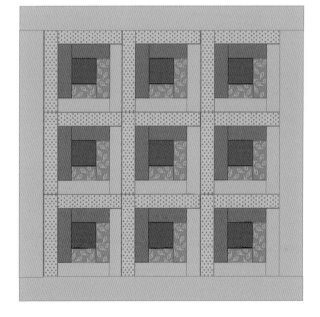

Mitered Borders

On some quilts a mitered border is really the finishing touch! Use a mitered border to achieve the look of a frame to set off your quilt or wall hanging.

1 Cut the borders.
- Cut borders ½" wider than the desired finished width. (We cut our borders 3"–4" wide, for a finished width of 2½"–3½".)
- Cut two borders a minimum of 8" longer than the side measurement of the quilt.
- Cut another two borders at least 8" longer than the top and bottom measurement of the quilt.

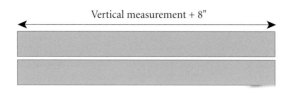

Vertical measurement + 8"

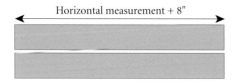

Horizontal measurement + 8"

2 Pin borders to the sides of the quilt top, right sides together, allowing equal amounts of excess strip length at each end of the quilt.

3 Stitch the borders to the quilt.
- Place a mark on the side borders ¼" from each corner of the quilt.
- Stitch from mark to mark using a ¼" seam.

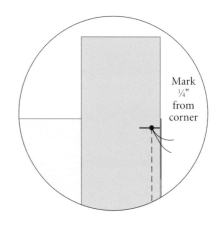

Mark ¼" from corner

4 Repeat, pinning and stitching borders to the top and bottom of the quilt, again stopping stitching ¼" from each corner and allowing 3"–4" extensions at each end.

5 Form the miters, working with one corner at a time.
  - Press the borders right side out to finished position.
  - Smooth one of the corner borders flat.

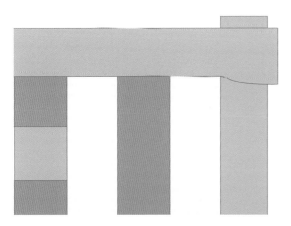

  - Fold the adjoining border, aligning the outer edges of the two border strips to create a 45° mitered corner. Press along the fold.

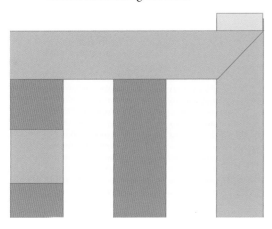

  - Pin the borders together at the mitered edge. Fold back the quilt top, exposing the wrong side and the press mark.

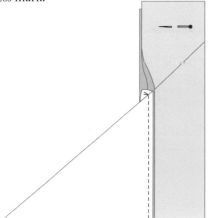

  - Stitch along the press mark, sewing to the point of the miter. Trim seam allowances to ¼".

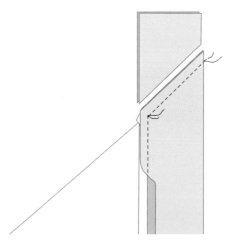

  - Press the seam open.

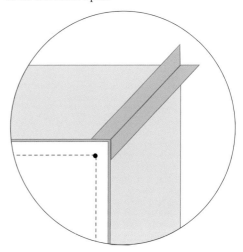

  - Repeat, mitering each corner.

Now you are ready to layer your quilt and add the backing and batting. See pp. 130–131.

Sampler Quilt

Combine several techniques in a sampler quilt of simple blocks that you've learned in chapters 1–4. Use the blocks that we have featured or pick your own favorites.

Missing Match-ups

The Missing Match-ups sampler quilt features two of each block, using a total of 16 blocks. It is a fun idea for a children's quilt because they can play a game finding the pairs.

Featured blocks:

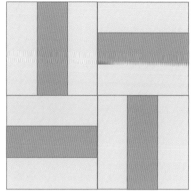

Roman Candle
See p. 38.

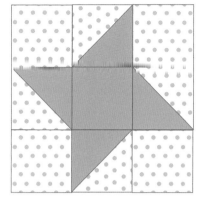

Friendship Star
See p. 69.

Snowball
See p. 76.

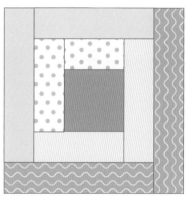

Simplified Log Cabin
See pp. 54–55.

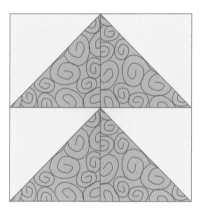

Flying Geese
See p. 67.

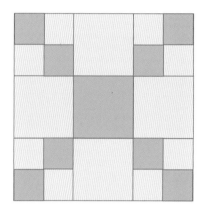

9-patch including a 4-patch
See pp. 22–23 and 28–29.

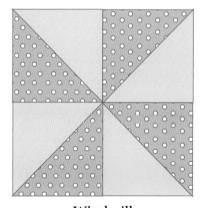

Windmill
See p. 66.

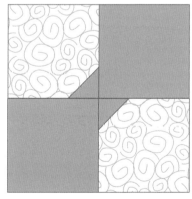

Bow Tie
See p. 78.

Other techniques featured:

- Sashing, see pp. 86–87.

- Cornerstones, see pp. 88–89.

- Borders, see pp. 90–91.

- Binding, see pp. 136–137.

chapter 6

Potpourri of Projects

The projects in this chapter will help you gain confidence as you begin to quilt. Quilters find enjoyment and relaxation in their hobby, and best of all—no fitting problems!

Placemats

Test your newfound quilting skills by creating these easy to quilt placemats. Directions and yardages are given for two-fabric 4-patch blocks, connected with solid blocks.

Once you know the basics, try other block options. Use three or four fabrics to make the blocks, or try different ways of arranging them. The possibilities are limited only by your imagination.

Finished Size: approximately 12" x 15"

Supplies Needed (Makes two placemats)
- ¼ yd. Fabric A (orange—blocks)
- ½ yd. Fabric B (green print—blocks and backing)
- ¼ yd. Fabric C (gold—blocks)
- ½ yd. batting
- Rotary cutter, mat, and ruler
- ¼" quilting foot, Patchwork Foot, or Little Foot®
- Curved Basting Pins, size 1

Instructions

Note: All seams are ¼" unless otherwise stated.

1. Cut fabrics.
   - Fabric A (orange): Cut two 2" crosswise strips (blocks).
   - Fabric B (green print):
     - Cut two 2" crosswise strips (blocks).
     - Cut one 12½" strip. Subcut two 12½" squares (backing). From remaining fabric, subcut two 3½" x 12½" strips (backing).

- Fabric C (gold): Cut two 3½" strips (solid blocks).
- Batting: Cut two 12½" x 15½" rectangles of batting.

2. Make twenty 4-Patch blocks using Fabrics A and B as detailed on pp. 22–23. Each placemat requires ten blocks.

3. Join 4-patch and solid blocks.
   - Stack 4-patch blocks, aligning colors.
   - Position a 3½" Fabric C strip, right side up, on the work surface.
   - Place a 4-patch block on top of the strip, right sides together and raw edges even, with the print at top left.
   - Stitch 4-patch to the strip with a ¼" seam allowance.
   - Place another 4-patch block on the strip, kissing the end to the first patch, with the print fabric at top left. Continue stitching.
   - Repeat until eight 4-patch blocks have been added to the strip.
   - Repeat, adding eight 4-patch blocks to the second 3½" Fabric C strip. Reserve remaining 4-patch blocks for later.

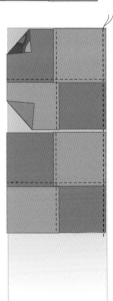

- Cut strip even with edges of 4-patch blocks, aligning raw edges with a quilting ruler to square the blocks.
- Press seam allowances toward the solid block.
- From the remainder of each 3½" Fabric C strip cut two 3½" squares.

4 Arrange the blocks for a placemat.
- Place two 4-patch/solid sets across and four sets down. Rotate the sets in opposite rows so that the 4-patch blocks are on the right in one row and the left in the next row.
- Alternate 4-patch blocks and 3½" Fabric C squares at the ends of the rows to complete the placemat layout.

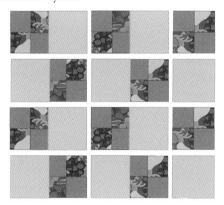

5 Stitch the placemat top.
- Join the two 4-patch/solid blocks in the first row, right sides together.
- Meet the two 4-patch/solid blocks in the second row, right sides together. "Kiss" them to the first row and continue chain stitching.

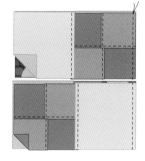

- Repeat chain stitching until 4-patch/solid blocks are joined in all four rows.
- Cut rows apart.
- Repeat, chain stitching to add the final block for each row.

- Press seams in one direction in the first row and in the opposite direction in the next row. Alternate direction in each remaining row.

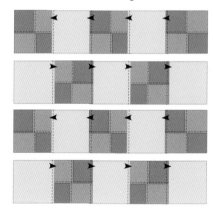

- Join rows, right sides together, aligning seam intersections to complete the top of the placemat. Press seams in one direction.

6 Repeat for the second placemat.

7 Complete the placemat.
- Create backing.
  - Pin the 3½" x 12½" backing strip to the 12½" backing square, right sides together.
  - Stitch 4" using a regular stitch length. Lock stitches, then use a basting stitch for 4". Lock stitches, and return to a regular stitch length for the remainder of the seam.

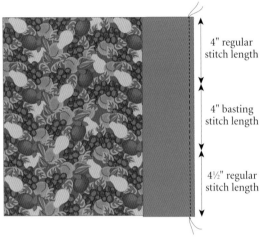

4" regular stitch length

4" basting stitch length

4½" regular stitch length

- Press seam flat and then open. Remove basting stitches.
- Trim ¼" diagonally from each of the four corners of the batting.
- Layer pieced placemat and batting.
  - Place pieced placemat over batting, right side up.
  - Pin through batting and pieced placemat on the solid blocks, using Curved Basting Pins. Keep pins at least 1" from edges. These pins are curved at just the right angle to make pinning your project a breeze!
- Stitch layers together.
  - Place backing on placemat, right sides together. Pin edges.

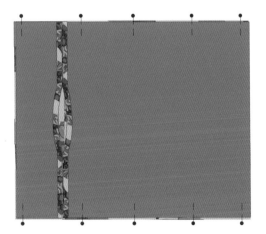

- Sew the two long edges of the placemat. Remove pins and press seam allowances flat.
- Trim batting from seam allowances.
- Wrap corners, pin and stitch the two short seams. Press seams flat, and then open.

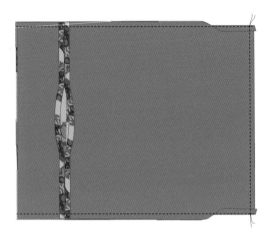

- Trim batting from seam allowances.
- Turn placemat right side out; press.
- Hand stitch the back opening closed.
- Tie the placemats with floss at block intersections, or bartack using your sewing machine. Remove Curved Basting Pins.

> **NOTE FROM NANCY**
>
> *Experiment with designs of your own, or use some of the examples on the following page as a guide.*

DESIGN DIVERSITY

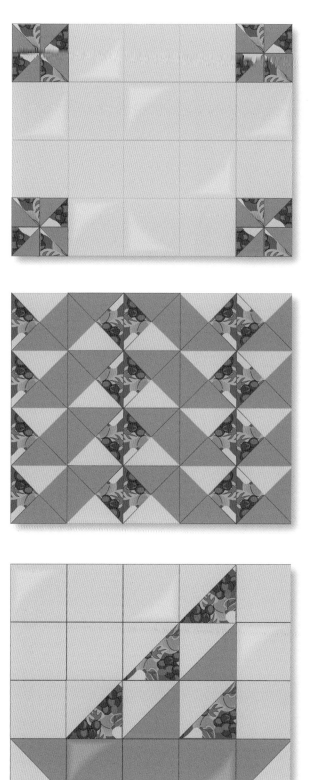
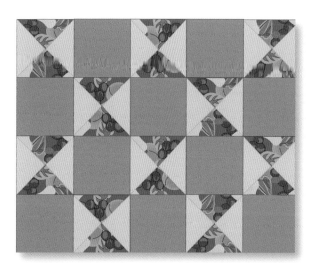
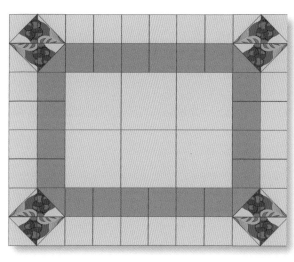
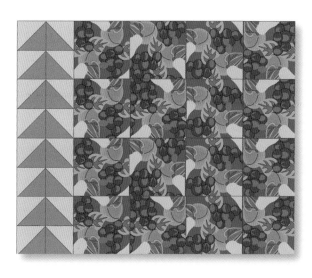

Table Runner

Create stratas, cut, and join blocks—easy methods that yield spectacular results! Using a flannel backing eliminates the need for batting. Easily quilt layers together by stitching in the ditch around the blocks. Make this table runner, and your next project could very easily be a quilt. You'll learn all the basics of quilt making! If you enjoy machine embroidery, the solid blocks are a perfect area to display some coordinating embroidery designs.

Finished Size: approximately 21" x 45"

Supplies Needed

- ⅞ yd. Fabric A (orange—strata, outer border, binding)
- ½ yd. Fabric B (green print—strata)
- ½ yd. Fabric C (gold—blocks)
- ⅛ yd. Fabric D (burgundy print—inner border)
- ⅔ yd. Fabric E (90" flannel—backing)
- Matching all-purpose thread
- Monofilament thread
- Sewer's Fix-it Tape
- Curved Basting Pins, size 1
- Binding and Hem Clips
- Rotary cutter, mat, and ruler
- Wash-away marking pen
- Machine Quilting Needle, size 90
- ¼" quilting foot, Little Foot®, or Patchwork Foot
- Walking Foot
- Optional: ¼" strip of paper-backed fusible web

Instructions

Note: All seams are ¼" unless otherwise stated.

1 Cut fabrics.
- Fabric A:
  - Cut four 2½" crosswise strips (strata).
  - Cut four 1½" crosswise strips (outer border).
  - Cut four 2½" crosswise strips (binding).
- Fabric B: Cut five 2½" crosswise strips (strata).
- Fabric C: Cut two 6½" crosswise strips; subcut into ten 6½" squares (blocks).
- Fabric D: Cut three 1" crosswise strips (border).

2 Prepare stratas.
- Strata 1: Arrange one strata with 2½" strips in the following order: Fabric A, Fabric B, and Fabric A.

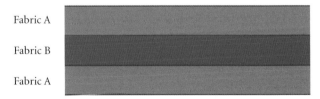

Fabric A
Fabric B
Fabric A

- Strata 2: Arrange two stratas with 2½" strips in the following order: Fabric B, Fabric A, and Fabric B.

Fabric B
Fabric A
Fabric B

Fabric B
Fabric A
Fabric B

- Join strips in each strata, right sides together, using ¼" seam allowances.
- Press seams flat. Press all seam allowances toward Fabric A.
- Subcut stratas into 2½" wide sections. Cut eleven sections from Strata 1 and twenty two sections from Strata 2.

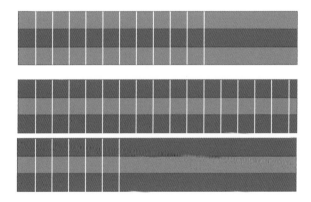

3 Assemble 9-patch blocks.
- Place a Strata 2 section on each side of a Strata 1 section.

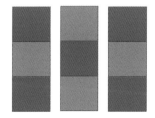

- Join sections, right sides together, matching seam intersections. Since seam allowances are all pressed toward Fabric A, intersections should easily align and stay in position for stitching.

- Press seams towards center.
- Repeat, preparing a total of eleven 9-patch blocks.

4 Complete the table runner blocks.
- Arrange three rows to form the table runner top, alternating 9-patch blocks with the 6½" Fabric C blocks.
  - Rows 1 and 3: Begin and end with 9-patch blocks.
  - Row 2: Begin and end with Fabric C blocks.
- Join blocks in each row, right sides together. Press seams in rows 1 and 3 in the same direction; press seams in row 2 in the opposite direction.

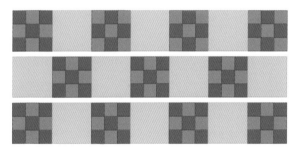

- Join rows, right sides together, matching block intersections, to form the table runner.

5 Add inner borders.
- Join Fabric D 1" border strips to two long edges of the pieced runner, right sides together. Press seams toward borders.

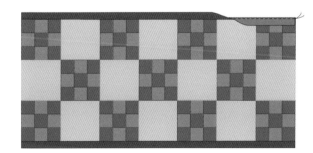

- Subcut remaining Fabric D border strip into two equal strips, each approximately 21" long. Join strips to short edges of the pieced runner, right sides together. Trim strips if necessary. Press seams toward borders.

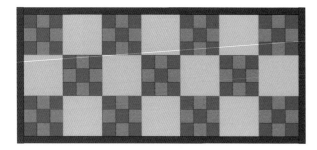

6 Add outer borders.
- Join Fabric A 1½" outer borders to two long edges of inner border, right sides together. Press seams toward borders.

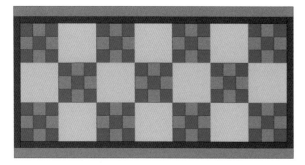

- Join Fabric A 1½" outer border strips to short edges of inner border, right sides together. Trim strips as necessary. Press seams toward borders.

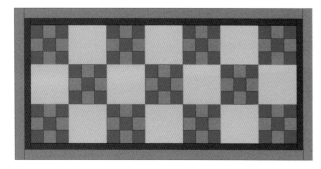

7 Layer, quilt, and bind the table runner following instructions in Finishing Finesse, beginning on p. 130. We used a flannel backing as it helps keep the finished table runner in place, and in this case, no batting is needed. Quilt as desired. We stitched in the ditch along seamlines to quilt the layers together; then stitched a scant ¼" from outer edges to secure the layers for the binding.

DESIGN DIVERSITY

Choose any of the blocks that you have learned so far to use in a table runner. Use a simple block that makes a 6½" finished square with ¼" seam allowances.

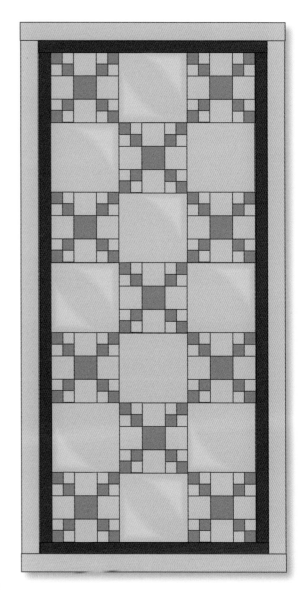

Casserole Carrier

16-patch blocks are the perfect size for turning this casserole carrier into an easy quilting project. Just place your casserole in the center and wrap it up! The insulated carrier is perfect for picnics or potluck dinners, since it has an additional inner pocket where you can insert a hot or cold pack to keep the temperature of your dish just right.

Finished Size: holds square/rectangular casserole up to 12"–13"

Supplies Needed:

- ⅓ yd. Fabric A (orange—strata)
- ⅝ yd. Fabric B (green print—strata and blocks)
- ¾ yd. Quilted Iron Quick (backing)
- 2 yd. 1" wide nylon webbing
- Matching all-purpose thread

- ¼ yd. hook and loop tape
- Rotary cutter, mat, and ruler
- Mini Korners Radial Rule® or saucer
- Pinking shears

Instructions:

Note: All seams are ¼" unless otherwise stated.

1 Cut fabrics.
- Fabric A: Cut three 3½" crosswise strips (strata). Subcut one of the strips into two 3½" x 21" strips.

Fabric A

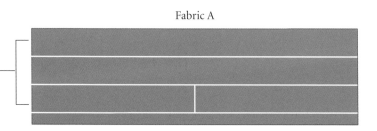

- Fabric B:
  - Cut two 3½" crosswise strips (strata).
  - Cut two 12½" squares (blocks).
  - Cut two 3½" x 17" strips from remaining fabric (strata).

- Quilted Iron Quick: Cut two 12½" x 36" rectangles (carrier backing).

Fabric B

2 Create a strata for the carrier's patchwork sections.
  - Arrange 42" long crosswise strips as follows: Fabric A, Fabric D, Fabric A, and Fabric B.
  - Join lengthwise edges of the four strips, right sides together, to form a strata.

  - Press seams toward the darker fabric.
  - Repeat, forming a similar strata with the short half strips (Fabric A strips will be longer than Fabric B strips.)

3 Subcut strata and complete four 16-patch blocks following instructions on pp. 34–35.

4 Join one 12½" block of Fabric B in the center of two 16-patch blocks for the top panel. Repeat to form a second identical section for the carrier base.

5 Complete top panel of the Casserole Carrier.
  - Center and stitch a 5½" loop side section of the hook and loop tape to the right side of one short edge of the panel.

- Center and stitch a 3" hook side of the hook and loop tape to the reflective side of one short edge of one Iron Quick section.

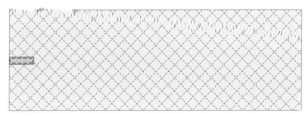

- Meet and pin completed top panel to Iron Quick, right sides together, checking to make sure hook and loop tape sections are at opposite ends. Round all four corners using the 1½" side of the Mini Korners Radial Rule™ or a saucer.

NOTE FROM NANCY

Square up and round the corners of the casserole carrier using your rotary cutter and the 45° line on the Radial Rule™.

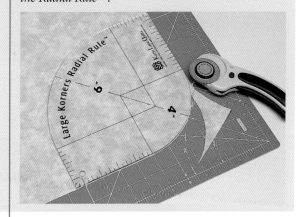

- Stitch a ¼" seam around outer edge, leaving a 6"–8" opening at the center of one long edge for turning.

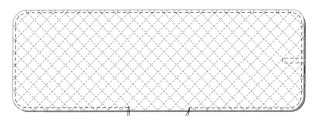

Casserole Carrier, *continued*

- Press seams open. Trim corners.

■ NOTE FROM NANCY

To reduce bulk when trimming, use a pinking shears. It's a great timesaver, since the zigzag edge of the shears removes excess fabric at the same time it trims the seam.

- Turn carrier top section right side out. Press edges. Edgestitch around outer edge of carrier, stitching opening closed at the same time.

- Quilt carrier section by stitching in the ditch along seamlines.

6 Complete the carrier base section.
- Center and stitch a 3" loop side of the hook and loop tape to the right side of one short edge of the carrier base.
- Center and stitch a 5½" hook side of the hook and loop tape to the reflective side of one short edge of the remaining Iron Quick section.

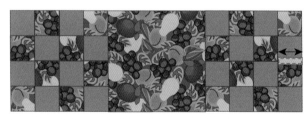

- Join carrier base and Iron Quick section, right sides together, with a ¼" seam, making sure hook and loop sections are at opposite ends. Quilt as for carrier top.

7 Attach handle to carrier base.
- Fold carrier base in half, meeting short ends. Mark center.
- Position webbing on quilted top, 3" from each long edge, meeting ends of the handle to the marked center. Pin handle in place.

- Measure 6" from each short edge. Mark from lengthwise edge to lengthwise edge. This indicates starting and stopping points for stitching the handles.
- Edgestitch each side of the handle webbing between the 6" markings.

- Stitch from edge to edge along the marked 6" line.

8 Join the casserole panels.
- Place the quilted sections right side up.
- Meet short ends of the top panel; mark the center.
- Place the carrier base at a right angle to the top panel, fabric side up, meeting center marks. Pin in place.

- Stitch along three edges of the unquilted center to secure the layers. Leave the remaining edge open for inserting a hot or cold pack.

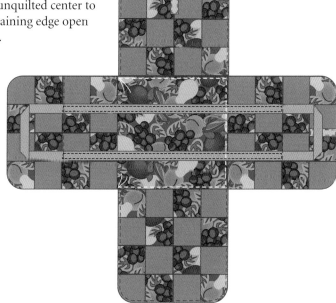

DESIGN DIVERSITY

Replace the 16-patch block with your favorite block and give the carrier a completely different look.

Tablecloth

Make your table festive in a flash! This tablecloth looks complicated, but it is simple to sew. The zigzag design is formed when the Triple Rail blocks are arranged in alternating directions and sewn together. Add borders and binding for a festive table topper.

Finished Size: approximately 56" square (6½" blocks)

Supplies Needed:
- 1⅛ yd. Fabric A (white print—strata and inner border)
- 1¼ yd. Fabric B (green print—strata and binding)
- 1½ yd. Fabric C (red print—strata and outer border)
- 1⅔ yd. white flannel, at least 60" wide (backing)
- Matching all-purpose thread
- Monofilament thread
- Sewer's Fix-it Tape
- Curved Basting Pins, size 1
- Binding and Hem Clips
- Rotary cutter, mat, and ruler
- Wash-away marking pen
- Machine Quilting Needle, size 90
- ¼" quilting foot, Little Foot®, or Patchwork Foot
- Walking Foot
- Optional: ¼" strip of paper-backed fusible web

Instructions:

Note: All seams are ¼" unless otherwise stated.

1 Cut fabrics to make 6½" finished blocks.
- Fabric A (white):
  - Cut eleven 2½" crosswise strips (strata).
  - Cut six 1½" crosswise strips (inner border).
- Fabric B (green):
  - Cut eleven 2½" crosswise strips (strata).
  - Cut six 2½" crosswise strips (binding).
- Fabric C (red):
  - Cut eleven 2½" crosswise strips (strata).
  - Cut six 3½" crosswise strips (outer border).

2 Stitch strips into strata.
- Join one 2½" strip each of Fabric A, Fabric B, and Fabric C for each of eleven strata.

Fabric C	
Fabric A	
Fabric B	

- Cut strata into 6½" blocks.

- Arrange eight rows, each containing eight blocks as shown. Join blocks in each row, right sides together. Press seams in alternate directions in adjacent rows.

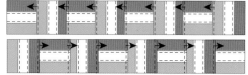

- Join rows, right sides together.

3 Piece border strips.
- Join short ends of Fabric A inner border strips, right sides together, with diagonal seams to reduce bulk.

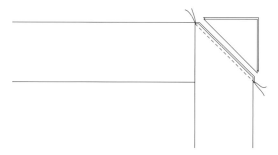

- Subcut two 1½" x 48½" strips and two 1½" x 50½" strips.
- Join short ends of Fabric C outer border strips, right sides together, with diagonal seams to reduce bulk.
- Subcut two 3½" x 50½" strips and two 3½" x 56½" strips.

4 Join border strips to the tablecloth.
- Add Fabric A (white) inner borders to the tablecloth.
  - Join 1½" x 48½" strips to top and bottom edges, right sides together. Trim any excess. Press seams toward borders.

  - Join 1½" x 50½" strips to left and right sides, right sides together. Trim any excess. Press seams toward borders.

Tablecloth, continued

- Add Fabric C (red) outer borders to the tablecloth.
  - Stitch 3½" x 50½" strips to top and bottom edges, right sides together. Trim any excess. Press seams toward borders.
  - Stitch 3½" x 56½" strips to left and right sides, right sides together. Trim any excess. Press seams toward borders.

DESIGN DIVERSITY

Make a tablecloth using your favorite 6½" finished blocks that include ¼" seam allowances. Vary the design by adding solid blocks between each pieced block. Countless options abound! Here are a few possibilities that you might want to try:

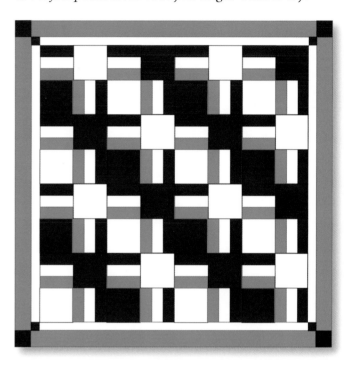

5 Layer, quilt, and bind the tablecloth following instructions in Finishing Finesse, beginning on p. 130. We used a flannel backing as it helps keep the finished tablecloth in place. In this instance, no batting is needed. Quilt as desired. We stitched in the ditch along seamlines plus a scant ¼" from outer edges to secure the layers for the binding.

Baby Quilt

If you're looking for an easy baby or toddler quilt, look no further! This framed square quilt has 36 blocks with two different color ways. Framed fabric is the same print as the border, but a different coloration. Make a few extra blocks for a matching pillow!

Finished Size: approximately 41" square (thirty-six 6" blocks plus borders)

Supplies Needed:
- ⅝ yd. Fabric A (white print—block centers)
- ⅝ yd. Fabric B (blue—frames and inner border)
- 1¾ yd. Fabric C (green—frames and backing)
- ⅝ yd. Fabric D (blue print—outer border and binding)
- 1¼ yd. batting or one crib size pkg. batting
- Matching all-purpose thread
- Monofilament thread
- Curved Basting Pins, size 1
- Binding and Hem Clips
- Rotary cutter, mat, and ruler
- Wash-away marking pen
- Machine Quilting Needle, size 90
- ¼" quilting foot, Little Foot®, or Patchwork Foot
- Walking Foot
- Optional: ¼" strip of paper-backed fusible web

Instructions:
Note: All seams are ¼" unless otherwise stated.

1 Cut fabrics for 6½" blocks.
- Fabric A (white print): Cut four 4½" crosswise strips (block centers).
- Fabric B (blue):
  - Cut ten 1½" strips (frames).
  - Cut four 1" strips (inner border).

- Fabric C (green):
  - Cut ten 1½" strips (frames).
  - Cut one 42" square (backing).
- Fabric D (blue print):
  - Cut four 2¼" strips (outer border).
  - Cut five 2¼" strips (binding).
- Cut a 45" square of batting.

2 Stitch strips together to form a strata.
- Place one 1½" strip of Fabric B (blue) over one strip of Fabric A (white print), right sides together. Stitch, joining lengthwise edges to form a strata. Repeat with a second strip each of Fabric B and Fabric A. Rotate each strata 180°.
- Place each strata over another strip of Fabric B, right sides together. Stitch, joining lengthwise edges, to complete the two stratas.

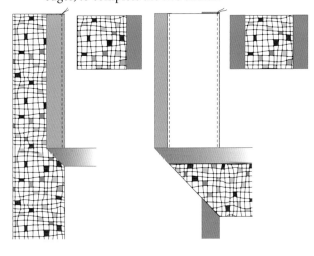

- Repeat using Fabric C (green) and Fabric A (white print) to form two additional stratas
- Press seams toward outer strips.

3 Subcut strata and complete blocks.

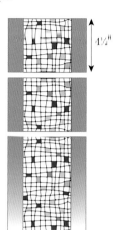

4¼"

- Straighten the edge of each strata as detailed on p. 20, aligning the ruler's horizontal markings with the cut edge of the strips.
- Subcut strata into 4½" sections. Stack and rotate sections. There should be 18 of each color.
- Place one 1½" strip of Fabric B on a work surface, right side up.
- Place a 4½" Fabric A/B section over the Fabric B strip, right sides together. Stitch, joining lengthwise edges, to complete three sides around the center blocks.
- Continue to chain stitch the sections until there are six sections on the strip. The most recently pieced part of the sections are at the top.

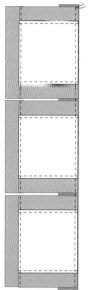

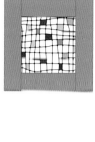

- Repeat the process, adding sections to Fabric C strips.

4 Complete quilt center.
- Arrange blocks, alternating colors as shown.
- Stitch six blocks together for each row.
- Join the six rows.

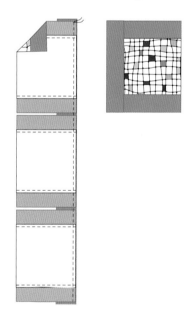

- Repeat with two more strips of Fabric B and six more 4½" sections for each strip.
- Cut sections apart and rotate 180°.
- Place three 1½" strips of Fabric B on the work surface, right side up. Place six sections on each, right sides together, joining the remaining edge to complete the center blocks.

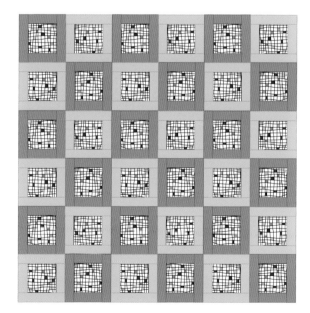

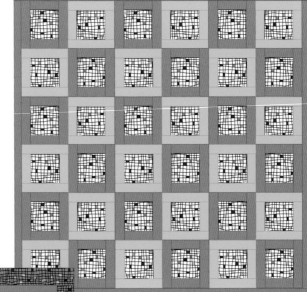

5 Add the 1" Fabric B inner borders.
  - Join inner border strips to the left and right edges of the quilt.
  - Join inner border strips to the top and bottom of quilt.

6 Add the 2¼" Fabric D outer borders.
  - Join outer border strips to the left and right edges of the quilt.
  - Join outer border strips to the top and bottom of the quilt.

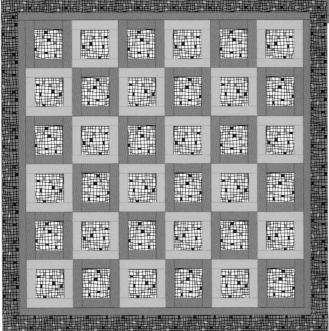

7 Layer the quilt backing, batting, and top following instructions on p. 130.

8 Machine quilt around blocks and borders using monofilament thread in the needle and all-purpose thread in the bobbin. Follow instructions on p. 132.

9 Bind the quilt edges following instructions on pp. 136–137.

DESIGN DIVERSITY

Choose thirty-six of your favorite 6½" blocks, or nine 12½" blocks (all of which include ¼" seam allowances), to create your very own version of this easy to sew baby quilt. Use all the same blocks and vary the colors, or add solid blocks to create an entirely different look.

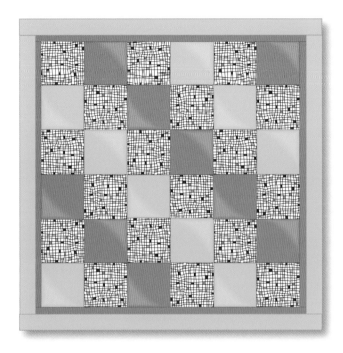
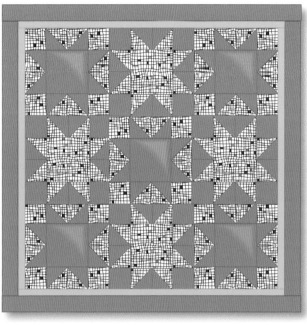
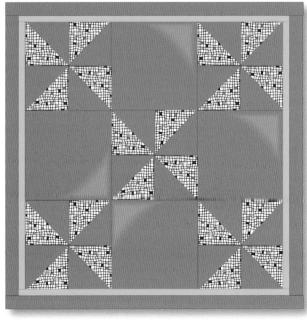
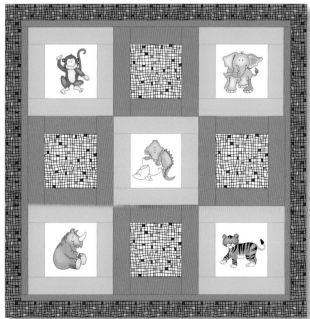

Embroidery designs from
Nancy Zieman's Safari Buddies

Framed Pillow

If you made a few extra blocks for the Baby Quilt, use them for this sweet and simple Framed Pillow. Or, make the frames with two different colorations, turning and arranging blocks as shown.

Finished Size: approximately 15½" square

Supplies Needed:
- ¼ yd. Fabric A (white print—block centers)
- ⅛ yd. Fabric B (blue—frames)
- ⅝ yd. Fabric C (green—frames and backing)
- ¼ yd. Fabric D (blue print—outer border)
- ½ yd. muslin
- ½ yd. batting
- Matching all-purpose thread
- Monofilament thread
- Rotary cutter, mat, and ruler
- Wash-away marking pen
- ¼" quilting foot, Little Foot®, or Patchwork Foot
- Walking Foot
- Polyester fiberfill

Instructions:

Note: All seams are ¼" unless otherwise stated.

1. Cut fabrics for 6½" blocks.
   - Fabric A (white print): Cut one 4½" crosswise strip (block centers).
   - Fabric B (blue): Cut two 1½" strips (frames).
   - Fabric C (green):
     - Cut two 1½" strips (frames).
     - Cut one 18" square (backing).
   - Fabric D (blue print): Cut two 2" strips (border).
   - Muslin: Cut two 18" squares.
   - Batting: Cut two 18" squares.

2. Stitch strips together to form a strata.
   - Lay one strip of Fabric C (green) over one strip of Fabric A (white print), right sides together. Stitch, joining lengthwise edges to form a strata. Rotate strips 180°.

- Lay strata over a second strip of Fabric C, right sides together. Stitch, joining lengthwise edge, to complete strata.

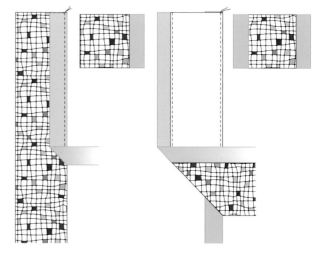

- Press seams toward outer strips.

3. Subcut strata and complete blocks.
   - Straighten the edge of each strata as detailed on p. 20, aligning the ruler's horizontal markings with the cut edge of the strips.
   - Subcut strata into four 4½" sections. Stack and rotate sections 90°.

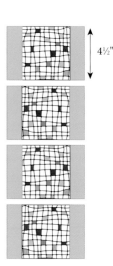

4½"

- Place one strip of Fabric B (blue) on a work surface, right side up.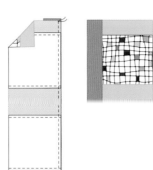
- Place a rotated 4½" section over the Fabric B strip, right sides together. Stitch, joining lengthwise edge. Continue to "kiss" and chain stitch additional 4½" sections until there are four sections on the strip. The most recently pieced part of the sections are at the top.
- Cut sections apart and rotate 180°.
- Lay second strip of Fabric B on the work surface, right side up. Chain stitch four sections to the strip, right sides together, to complete the center blocks.

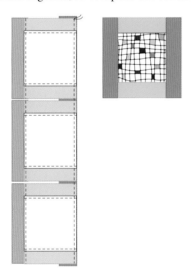

4 Complete pillow center.
- Arrange blocks, alternating colors as shown.

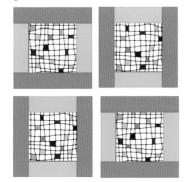

- Stitch two blocks together for each row.
- Join the two rows.

5 Add the 2" Fabric D border.
- Join border strips to the sides of the pillow.

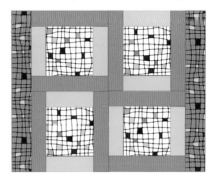

- Join border strips to the top and bottom of pillow.

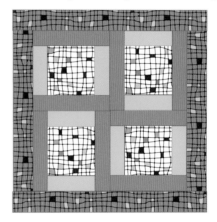

6 Quilt the 18" backing.
- Layer 18" muslin, batting, and backing sections.
- Mark gridlines 3" apart vertically and horizontally.
- Stitch through all layers, following marked lines.

7 Quilt the pillow top.
- Layer 18" muslin, batting, and pillow top sections.
- Quilt through all layers, stitching in the ditch of the quilt block seams, using a monofilament thread in the needle and all-purpose thread in the bobbin.

8 Trim muslin and backing even with the pillow top.

9 Complete the pillow.
- Place pillow top and backing right sides together.
- Join top and backing using a ¼" seam, leaving a 5" opening on one side for turning. Optional: Wrap corners; see p. 100.
- Trim corners close to stitching. Turn right side out.
- Stuff pillow through the 5" opening. Stitch opening closed by hand.

Wall Hanging

Use any 12½" block with ¼" seam allowances to make a simply delightful wall hanging! We used half-square triangles to create a star with a windmill in the center. Adjust the size of the borders to make a coordinating pillow in a size of your choice.

Wall Hanging by Karen Zilke

Finished Size: approximately 20½" square

Supplies Needed:

- ¼ yd. Fabric A (cream—squares and border)
- ½ yd. Fabric B (green—squares, border, and binding)
- ⅓ yd. Fabric C (cherry print—squares and border)
- ⅔ yd. muslin (backing and rod pockets)
- Matching all-purpose thread
- Monofilament thread
- Rotary cutter, mat, and ruler
- Quilt hanger
- Optional: Inkjet fabric sheet, 05 Pigma Pen, and Steam-A-Seam 2® for label

Instructions:

Note: All seams are ¼" unless otherwise stated.

1 Cut fabrics.
- Fabric A (cream):
  - Cut one 3½" strip (squares): Subcut one 3½" x 15" strip, two 1¼" x 12½" strips, and two 1¼" x 14" strips (squares and first border).

  - Cut one 3⅞" strip (half-square triangles).
- Fabric B (green):
  - Cut one 3⅞" strip (half-square triangles).
  - Cut two 1¼" strips. Subcut two 1¼" x 14" strips and two 1¼" x 15½" strips (second border).
  - Cut three 2½" crosswise strips (binding).
- Fabric C (cherry print):
  - Cut one 3⅞" strip (half-square triangles).
  - Cut two 3" strips. Subcut each into one 3" x 15½" strip and one 3" x 20½" strip (third border).
- Muslin:
  - Cut one 23" square (backing).
  - Cut two 3" x 8" rod pockets for decorative hanger as shown on p. 123.
- Batting: Cut one 23" square.

2 Cut squares.
- Cut four 3½" squares from the 3½" x 15" strip of Fabric A (cream).
- Cut four 3⅞" squares from the 3⅞" strip of Fabric A (cream).
- Cut six 3⅞" squares from the 3⅞" strip of Fabric B (green).
- Cut two 3⅞" squares from the 3⅞" strip of Fabric C (cherry print).

3 Stitch half-square triangles.
   - Place four 3⅞" squares of Fabric A on top of four 3⅞" squares of Fabric B, right sides together. Stitch half-square triangles following instructions on pp. 64–65.
   - Place two 3⅞" squares of Fabric B on top of two 3⅞" squares of Fabric C, right sides together. Stitch half-square triangles following instructions on pp. 64–65.

4 Arrange squares as illustrated.

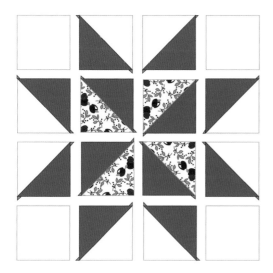

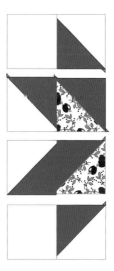

6 Repeat, chaining the second pair of blocks in each row.

7 Join block pairs for each row.

8 Join rows to complete the 12½" block.

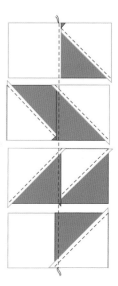

5 Meet and chain stitch the first pair of blocks in each row, right sides together. Press seams in opposite directions in adjacent rows.

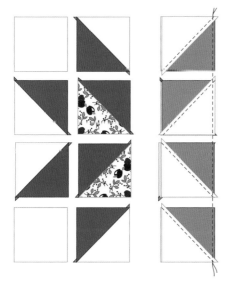

9 Add borders.

- First border (Fabric A):
  - Stitch 1¼" x 12½" border strips to the left and right edges of the block. Press seams toward borders.

- Second border (Fabric B):
  - Stitch 1¼" x 14" border strips to the left and right edges of the block. Press seams toward borders.

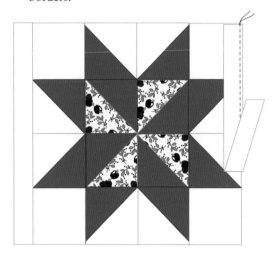

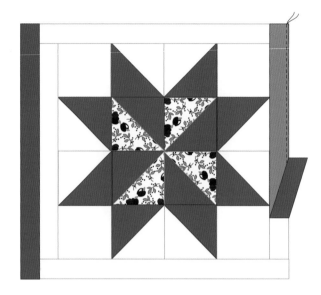

- Stitch 1¼" x 14" border strips to the top and bottom of the block. Press seams toward borders.

- Stitch 1¼" x 15½" border strips to the top and bottom of the block. Press seams toward borders.

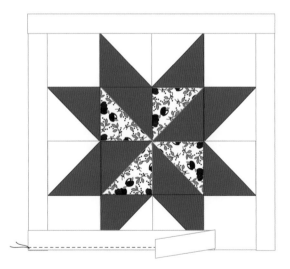

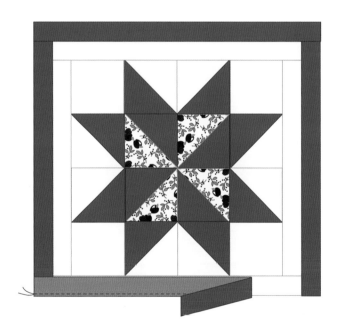

- Third (outer) border (Fabric C):
  - Stitch 3" x 15½" border strips to the left and right edges of the block. Press seams toward borders.
  - Stitch 3" x 20½" border strips to the top and bottom of the block. Press seams toward borders.

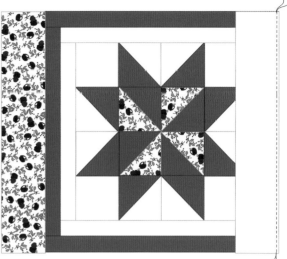

10 Square up the wall hanging following instructions on p. 130.

11 Layer the wall hanging with the muslin right side down on work surface, batting in the center, and wall hanging top, right side up, on top of the batting. Follow instructions for layering and pinning on pp. 130–131.

12 Quilt the layers together by stitching in the ditch with monofilament thread. Follow instructions on p. 132.

13 Create two rod pockets using the 3" x 8" strips of muslin and the instructions on p. 137. Sew the rod pockets to the top edge of the wrong side of the wall hanging, positioning them about 1" from each side.

14 Bind the quilt using two Fabric B 2½" strips, following the instructions on pp. 136–137.

15 Complete the rod pocket by stitching the lower edge in place following instructions on p. 137.

16 Create your own label or photocopy and print one of the labels on pp. 139–141 on an inkjet fabric sheet to use on the back of your wall hanging. Stitch label on by hand or fuse it in place with a paper-backed fusible web, such as Steam-A-Seam 2®.

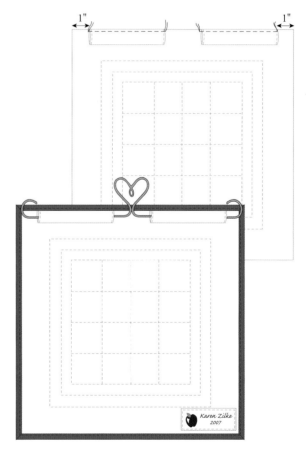

Summer Serenity Quilt

This lovely "Summer Serenity" quilt is a half-square triangle sampler including Windmills, Flying Geese, and simple variations of Bow Ties and Squares. We also added sashing, borders, and cornerstones as detailed in Chapter 5. Brighten your boudoir with this floral beauty!

Finished Size: approximately 72½" x 90½"

Supplies Needed

- 2¼ yd. Fabric A (lg. blue floral—blocks, outer border, and binding)
- ½ yd. Fabric B (sm. blue floral—blocks and cornerstones)
- ¼ yd. Fabric C (lg. pink floral—blocks)
- ⅔ yd. Fabric D (sm. pink floral—blocks and cornerstones)
- ½ yd. Fabric E (lg. green floral—blocks)
- 1⅝ yd. Fabric F (green paisley—sashing and inner border)
- 1½ yd. Fabric G (light yellow—blocks)
- 5¼ yd. Fabric H (lg. yellow floral—backing)
- 2 yd. low loft 90" wide batting
- Matching all-purpose thread
- Matching cotton quilting thread or monofilament thread
- Rotary cutter, mat, and ruler
- Quilt clips such as Jaws™ or Quick Clips
- Curved Basting Pins, size 1
- Kwik Klip™

Instructions

Note: All seams are ¼" unless otherwise stated.

1. Cut fabrics.
   - Fabric A (lg. blue floral):
     - Cut eight 2½" crosswise strips (binding).
     - Cut seven 6½" crosswise strips (outer borders).

   Note: Spray starch the remaining fabric before cutting. The spray starch helps stabilize the fabric and makes it easier to draw diagonal stitching lines for each half-square triangle block.

     - Cut one 6⅞" crosswise strip. Subcut six 6⅞" squares (blocks).
   - Fabric B (sm. blue floral): Cut two 6⅞" crosswise strips.
     - Subcut eight 6⅞" squares (blocks).
     - Subcut four 3½" squares (inner cornerstones).
   - Fabric C (lg. pink floral): Cut one 6⅞" crosswise strip. Subcut six 6⅛" squares (blocks).
   - Fabric D (sm. pink floral):
     - Cut one 6½" crosswise strip. Subcut four 6½" squares (large cornerstones).
     - Cut two 6⅞" crosswise strips. Subcut eight 6⅞" squares (blocks).

- Fabric E (lg. green floral): Cut two 6⅞" crosswise strips. Subcut eight 6⅞" squares (blocks).
- Fabric F (green paisley): Cut fifteen 3½" crosswise strips (sashing and inner border strips).
- Fabric G (yellow):
  - Cut six 6⅞" crosswise strips. Subcut thirty-six 6⅞" squares (blocks).
  - Cut one 6½" crosswise strip. Subcut two 6½" squares (blocks).
- Fabric H (lg. yellow floral): Divide the 5¼ yd. of fabric into two sections, each approximately 42" x 94½". Join 94½" edges using a ¼" seam allowance (backing).

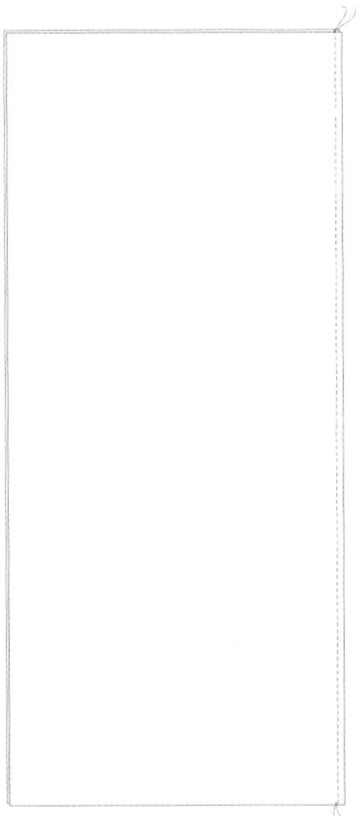

Backing

2 Make half-square triangles as indicated for each design, following general instructions on pp. 64–65. Then arrange squares following instructions for each design.

Flying Geese (6½" x 12½" half blocks)
- Meet eight 6⅞" Fabric E (lg. green floral) squares to eight Fabric G yellow squares, right sides together. Stitch along seamlines and cut squares apart on marked center line to create 16 half-square triangles for the Flying Geese.
- Press seams toward darker fabric.
- Meet the right sides of each set of two half-square triangles, green triangles together, to create the Flying Geese for row one.

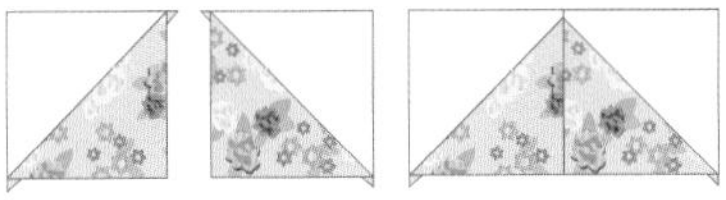

Repeat for bottom row.
- Cut four 3½" x 6½" sashing strips from Fabric F (green paisley). Join sashing strips to Flying Geese to complete top and bottom rows as illustrated.

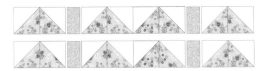

Hour Glass (12½" blocks)
- Construct two Hour Glass blocks using two 6⅞" Fabric D (small pink floral) squares and two 6⅞" Fabric G (yellow) squares for the half-square triangles, plus two 6½" Fabric G (yellow) blocks as detailed on p. 68.
- Repeat, making two Hour Glass blocks using two 6⅞" Fabric B (sm. blue floral) squares and two 6⅞" Fabric G (yellow) squares for the half-square triangles, plus two 6½" Fabric G (yellow) blocks.
- Set blocks aside for use with Windmills.

Make two of each coloration

Windmill (12½" blocks)
- Construct four Windmill blocks. Make half-square triangles by joining four 6⅞" Fabric A (lg. blue floral) squares to four 6⅞" Fabric G (yellow) squares plus four 6⅞" Fabric B (sm. blue floral) squares to four 6⅞" Fabric G (yellow) squares. Follow directions for making Windmills on p. 66, using two of each coloration per block.
- Repeat, constructing four Windmill blocks joining four 6⅞" Fabric C (lg. pink floral) squares to four 6⅞" Fabric G (yellow) squares plus four 6⅞" Fabric D (small pink floral) squares to four 6⅞" Fabric G (yellow) squares.
- Arrange completed Windmill and reserved Hour Glass blocks in rows 2 and 4, as shown. Reserve remaining four Windmills for the center section.

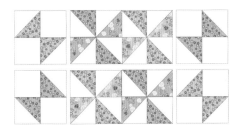

- Subcut four 3½" x 12½" sashing strips from Fabric F (green paisley). Attach sashing to Hour Glass and Windmill blocks as shown in rows 2 and 4.

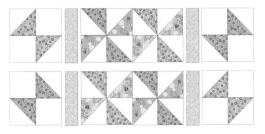

Square Within a Square (Center Blocks)

- Construct two pink combination Square Within a Square blocks.
  - Make half-square triangles as detailed on pp. 64–65 using two 6⅞" Fabric D (small pink floral) squares and two 6⅞" Fabric G (yellow) squares.
  - Repeat, making a second set of half-square triangles using two 6⅞" Fabric C (lg. pink floral) squares and two 6⅞" Fabric G (yellow) squares.
  - Combine the half-square triangles as shown to make two 12½" Square Within a Square blocks.

- Construct two blue combination Square Within a Square blocks.
  - Make half-square triangles using two 6⅞" Fabric B (small blue floral) squares and two 6⅞" Fabric G (yellow) squares.
  - Repeat, making a second set of half-square triangles using two 6⅞" Fabric A (lg. blue floral) squares and two 6⅞" Fabric G (yellow) squares.
  - Combine the half-square triangles as shown to make two 12½" Square Within a Square blocks.

- Join the pink and blue Square Within a Square blocks, alternating colors for the center section of the quilt.

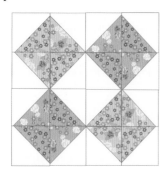

- Join reserved pink and blue Windmills as shown to make the left and right sides of the center section.

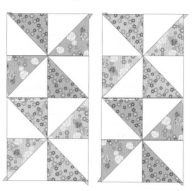

- Subcut two 3½" x 24½" sashing strips from Fabric F strips. Join sashing strips to Windmills and Square Within a Square blocks as illustrated.

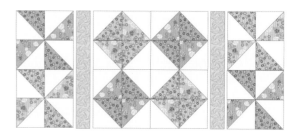

3 Add horizontal sashing.
- Measure completed rows and subcut Fabric F sashing strips according to that measurement. Sashing strips will need to be pieced to measure approximately 3½" x 54½" each.
- Sew the sashing to the completed rows as illustrated. Press seams toward sashing.

4 Add inner border and cornerstones.
  - Measure the width and length of the quilt top through the center of the quilt, horizontally and vertically. The measurement will be approximately 54½" x 72½".
  - Piece a 3½" Fabric F inner border strip for each side of the quilt. Cut left and right strips about 72½" long and top and bottom strips approximately 54½" long.
  - Pin and sew left and right inner borders to the quilt top, right sides together. Press seams toward borders.
  - Add Fabric B (sm. blue floral) cornerstones to the ends of the top and bottom inner border strips, right sides together.
  - Pin and sew top and bottom borders to quilt top. Press seams toward borders.

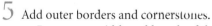

5 Add outer borders and cornerstones.
  - Remeasure width and length of the quilt top through the center of the quilt, horizontally and vertically. Measurement will be approximately 60½" x 78½".
  - Piece two 6½" Fabric A (lg. blue floral) outer border strips for each side of the quilt. Cut left and right strips about 78½" long, and top and bottom strips approximately 60½" long, or as measured above.
  - Pin and sew left and right outer borders to the quilt top, right sides together. Press seams toward dark fabric.

- Add the Fabric D (sm. pink floral) cornerstones to the ends of the top and bottom outer border strips, right sides together.
- Pin and sew top and bottom borders to quilt top. Press seams toward dark fabric.

6 Layer and pin quilt.
- Layer quilt on a flat surface or quilting frame. See pp. 130–131 for layering technique.
  - Place Fabric H (lg. yellow floral) right side down on flat surface or quilting frame.
  - Center batting over Fabric H.
  - Center the quilt top, right side up, over the batting.
- Pin quilt layers together using Curved Basting Pins, and the Kwik Klip™ for ease of closure, if desired. See p. 131 for information on using the Kwik Klip™.

7 Quilt through all layers using your favorite technique. See pp. 132–135 for various quilting techniques.

NOTE FROM NANCY
Use quilt clips such as Jaws™ to keep your quilt neatly rolled when machine quilting and to keep it clean and secure when you are not working on it. Just open and twist to position the Jaws on the quilt roll.

8 Bind the quilt using eight Fabric A (lg. blue floral) binding strips, following the instructions on pp. 136–137.

9 Create your own label, or photocopy and print one of the labels on pp. 139–141 on an inkjet fabric sheet to use on the back of your quilt. Stitch label on the quilt by hand or fuse in place with a paper-backed fusible web, such as Steam-A-Seam 2®.

COLOR AND DESIGN DIVERSITY

Use Bow Tie blocks throughout rows 2 and 4 mirroring the positions of the center two. Also use Bow Tie blocks in the center, with the top two facing one direction and the bottom two in the opposite direction. Or, make your own favorite half-square triangle combinations.

Finishing Finesse

A quilt is generally composed of a top, a layer of batting, and a backing fabric. The following techniques are the same regardless of whether you're making a quilt, wall hanging, table runner, or other quilted project.

Squaring the Project

Squaring a quilted project gives it a professional look. With quilted wall hangings, squaring also makes the project hang more evenly. Square individual blocks first, then join the blocks, adding sashing, cornerstones, borders, and binding as detailed on pp. 86–93 and 136–139.

> ■ **NOTE FROM NANCY**
> *Use The Block Marker™ to perfectly align sides and corners of your quilt blocks before joining the blocks. It's a must-have quilting notion!*
>
>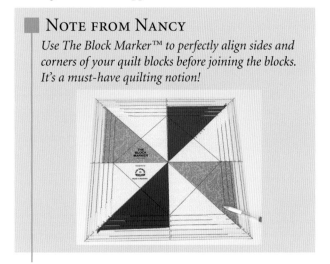

- Square the quilt top. Measure the project from top to bottom, side to side, and corner to corner to ensure it is square.

- Trim edges as needed to achieve square corners and uniform measurements.
- Clip any loose threads and give the quilt top a final pressing.

Layering the Quilt

- Cut backing fabric and batting approximately 3" larger than the quilt top on all sides.
- Place the backing, wrong side up, on a firm clean surface.
- Securely tape the backing to the surface, using Sewer's Fix-it Tape or masking tape.

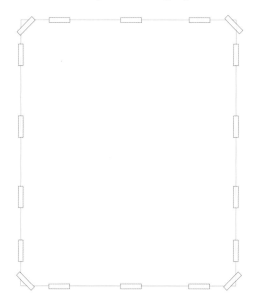

- Choose the batting best suited for your quilt using information on p. 11.

> ■ **NOTE FROM NANCY**
> *For some projects, such as table runners and table-cloths, batting may not be essential. Use a flannel backing instead. It keeps the finished project in place, and is especially nice for projects where a minimum amount of loft is desired.*

- Center the batting over the backing and smooth the surface so that it lies flat.

- Center the quilt top, right side up, over the batting or flannel backing.

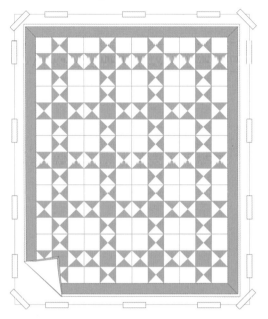

- Pin quilt layers together using size 1 Curved Basting Pins. Start pinning at the center and work toward the outer edges.
- Place pins 3"–4" apart and no closer than ½" from seams to allow room for the presser foot when machine quilting.

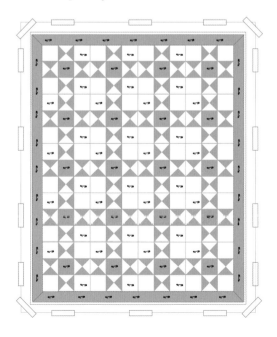

- You can save time and effort by spray basting your quilt with a temporary adhesive basting spray, such as Generations™ Quilt Basting Spray or Sulky® KK2000™. This acid-free adhesive spray enables you to layer top, batting, and backing without pins or hand basting. It holds fabric firmly, yet fabric can be easily repositioned.
- Remove the tape once the pin or adhesive basting is complete.
- Baste a scant ¼" from outer edges.

- Trim edges of backing and batting even with quilt top.

Quilting Options

There are several quilting options. Among them are hand quilting, tying, and various methods of machine quilting. Especially for beginners, machine quilting and tying are faster and easier.

Machine Quilting Methods

Make sure your sewing machine is in good repair, clean, and has the tension adjusted before you begin your quilting project. Always quilt from the center to the outside of your quilt to avoid shifting and bunching. The following are common machine quilting techniques.

Stitch in the Ditch

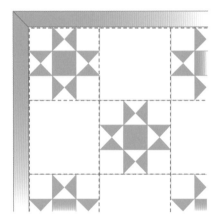

Stitching in the ditch follows the seamlines (blocks, borders, sashing, etc.) in a design. You have an easy guide to follow as you stitch.

1 Adjust the sewing machine for machine quilting.
   - Use a medium length straight stitch with a balanced tension.
   - Thread the top of the machine with cotton thread matched to the fabric. Or, use a monofilament thread. Available in clear and smoke colorations, monofilament thread blends with a wide variety of fabric colorations, making thread changes unnecessary.
   - Insert a machine quilting needle.
   - If possible, adjust the machine to stop with the needle in "down" position.

- Use a Walking Foot to feed fabric evenly. It's important to prevent the layers of the quilt sandwich from shifting, and a Walking Foot helps feed all the layers through the machine smoothly and evenly.
- Machine quilt, stitching in the well of the seamlines with matching or monofilament thread so that stitches are less conspicuous.
- Stitch around each pieced block, as well as along the border seams.

Echo Quilting

Echo quilting follows the contour of one or more of the elements of the quilt design. It helps add depth and dimension to a project.

1 Adjust machine as detailed at top left.

2 Machine quilt, stitching about ¼" from the pieced or appliqué design.

3 Continue to echo that stitching in ¼" increments that move outward.

> ### NOTE FROM NANCY
> *Use your presser foot to help achieve uniformly spaced rows of stitching. After completing one row of stitching, guide the edge of the presser foot along the previous row of stitching.*

Grid Line Quilting

Grid line quilting is uniformly spaced throughout the project. It's almost like stitching a checkerboard.

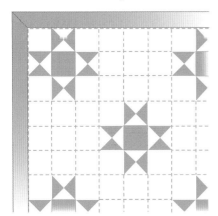

1 Adjust the machine as indicated on p. 132. Use a Quilting Guide Bar with the Walking Foot to keep rows of stitching an equal distance apart. Follow instructions that came with the foot for attaching the Walking Foot and Guide Bar.

NOTE FROM NANCY

Adjust the Quilting Guide Bar for the width of the grid you plan to stitch. After stitching the first row, guide the bar along the previous row of stitching.

2 Machine quilt in straight lines vertically and horizontally, forming a grid. Work from the center toward outer edges. You may want to mark your quilting lines with a removable fabric pen or pencil, such as a mechanical marking pencil, to keep the rows even if you are not using a Quilting Guide Bar.

NOTE FROM NANCY

The "lead" for ultra fine point mechanical pencils intended for marking fabric isn't lead at all—it's compressed chalk. Markings can be easily and completely removed using the eraser and bristled pen end.

Stencil Quilting

Commercially available stencils can provide stitching guides for machine quilting designs. Some stencils are made of plastic or Templar; transfer those design to the quilt with a fabric marker. Other machine quilting designs are printed onto paper.

1 Adjust machine as indicated on p. 132.

2 When using a commercial plastic stencil, transfer the stencil design to the project with a fabric marking pen or pencil. Machine quilt following the traced design.

3 If you have drawn your own stencil, traced a design onto paper, or selected a preprinted paper stencil, stitch the motif through the paper, following the outline design.
   - Hold the paper in position on the project by using a temporary quilt basting spray. No pins or basting stitches are required, yet the paper can be repositioned before sewing.
   - Stitch directly over the paper, following the design.
   - Remove paper after stitching is completed.

NOTE FROM NANCY

Although the needle perforates the paper during machine quilting and makes removing the paper relatively easy, here's another way to simplify the process. Run the tip of a seam ripper, awl, or stiletto along the stitching line. The paper readily separates from the stitching.

Quilting Options, *continued*

Stippling or Meandering

This technique requires free-motion stitching of small puzzle-like designs, with stitches never crossing or touching one another. Stippling typically refers to designs stitched closer together than meandering.

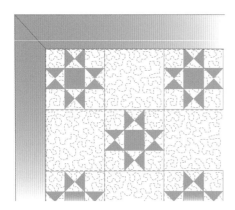

1 Set your machine up for free-motion quilting. Follow these general guidelines, but refer to your instruction manual for specifics for your machine.
- Lower or cover the feed dogs. You, rather than the feed dogs, control the motion of the fabric.
- Replace the conventional presser foot with a Darning Foot or Big Foot. These feet provide good surface contact with the quilt fabric and keep the fabric close to the bed of the machine. Because the feet are transparent, they allow you to clearly see where you're stitching.

Darning Foot   Big Foot

- Use a cotton thread for both the bobbin and the needle, matching the color to the fabric. Or, use monofilament thread in the needle and cotton or polyester thread matched to the backing in the bobbin.
- Use a machine quilting needle.

- Adjust tension as needed. If the same thread is used in both the needle and the bobbin, use a balanced tension. If the top thread is different than that in the bobbin, loosen the top tension by two numbers or notches to prevent the bobbin thread from being drawn to the top of the fabric.

2 Stipple the quilt.
- It's not necessary to mark the design. Practice on scraps before working on your project, using the same combination of top fabric, batting, and backing as in the actual project. You'll find your stippling gets better with practice.
- Position your hands on both sides of the presser foot to hold the fabrics in place and guide them during stitching. You may want to wear rubber fingers (available from an office supply store) to stabilize the fabric.

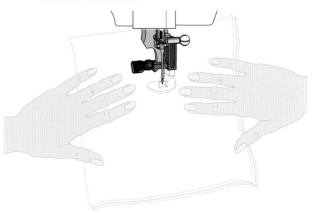

- Begin in the center of the quilt and work toward outer edges. Stitch in small 1"–2" sections.
- Develop a rhythm by moving the fabric slowly and stitching at a medium to fast speed.
- Remove any pins as you come to them.
- Maintain the same stitch intensity over the entire quilt surface. If some portions of the project are heavily stitched and others are lightly stitched, the finished project will not be flat or square.

NOTE FROM NANCY

Stippling takes practice, but I find it to be very relaxing and enjoyable. Whenever possible, position the bulk of the fabric to the left of the machine. With large projects, you may want to roll the edge of the quilt toward the middle and secure it with quilt clips. Be sure to support the fabric on a table or flat surface as you stitch so there is no strain, which could distort the fabric.

Tying

Tying the quilt project is a good choice when using a thick batting or when you would like to finish the quilting process quickly. Decorative threads can add color and charm to a tied project.

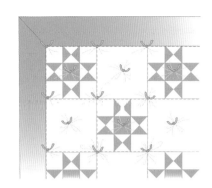

1 Use a long needle with an eye large enough for inserting the thread or yarn used for tying your project.

2 Mark the project at regular intervals, establishing a grid for the tying. In general, ties should be no farther apart than the width of your fist.

3 Tie the project with a single or double strand of perle cotton, narrow ribbon, or yarn.

Professional Longarm Quilting

If you don't have time to quilt your project yourself—or if you'd like to turn that task over to someone else with more experience—consider having your project professionally quilted. Professional quilting is popular, and can add a lot to a simple pieced quilt design, especially if the quilter has a computerized machine—the designs are almost limitless! Check with your local quilt shop, online, or in quilt related magazines for a recommendation. Ask to see samples of their work. Having a project professionally quilted does add to its cost, but think about all the time you've saved, and enjoy the spectacular results.

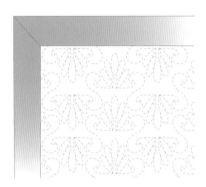

Binding

Binding finishes off the edges of your project and can add a small border of color, or blend with the final border. Square the quilt as detailed on p. 130 before adding the binding.

1 Measure around the outside unfinished edges of the project and add approximately 7" to that measurement to determine the length of the binding. A typical width for binding is 2¼"–2½". This makes a binding with a finished width of ¼"–⅜".

2 Prepare the binding.
- Cut enough crosswise fabric strips to equal the length of the binding. Join the strips together at short ends, right sides together, with diagonal seams to reduce bulk. Trim seams to ¼"; press seams open.
- Cut one end of the strip at a 45° angle using a rotary cutter, mat, and quilting ruler. Fold in ¼" at trimmed end. Optional: Press a ¼" strip of paper-backed fusible web to the folded-under edge of the binding. Leave the paper backing in place.

- Fold binding in half, wrong sides together, meeting lengthwise edges. Press.

- Mark the right side of the project ¼" from each corner.

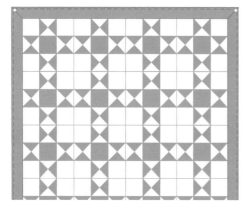

3 Bind the outer edges of the project.
- Meet the angle-cut end of the binding (the end with the paper-backed fusible web) to the right side of the project, meeting raw edges and starting in the center of one side. Start on a side other than the top edge to minimize bulk.
- Stitch binding to the project with a scant ¼" seam, beginning 4" down from the end of the binding and stopping at the marked point at the first corner. Lock stitches.

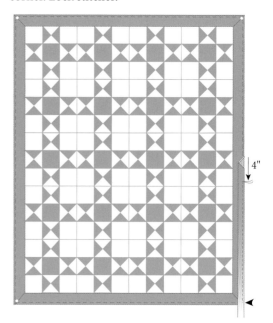

- Fold binding up, creating a 45° angle, aligning the cut edge of the binding with the cut edge of the project.

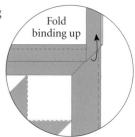

- Fold the binding down, meeting the binding fold to the top edge of the project and the binding cut edge to side edges. Stitch a ¼" seam on the side, starting at the folded edge.
- Repeat at remaining corners.

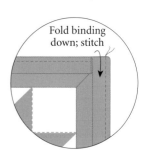

- To join binding ends: Remove paper backing from fusible web. Insert free end of the binding inside the beginning of the binding so binding is smooth and even with the edge of the project. Unfold binding; trim excess.
- Press to fuse binding ends together. Refold binding and stitch the remainder of the binding seam.

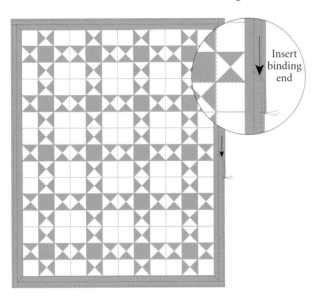

- Fold and press binding away from the project.
- Fold binding to the wrong side, covering stitching line and tucking in corners to miter them. Pin, or secure with Binding and Hem Clips.

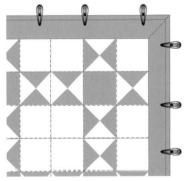

- Stitch in the ditch, sewing in the well of the binding seamlines on the front. Or, slipstitch the binding in place on the back of the project.

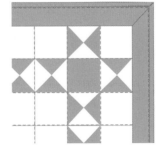

Rod Pocket

Using a rod pocket is one of several ways to hang a wall hanging. Although there are many different methods for making a rod pocket, this is our favorite. It's easy and fast to construct.

1 Cut a rod pocket from muslin or backing fabric 3" wide, and a little narrower than the top of your wall hanging.

2 Clean finish the 3" edges of the rod pocket strip by turning under ¼" on each edge twice. Press and stitch.

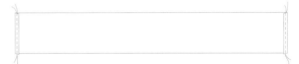

3 Press rod pocket in half, wrong sides together, meeting cut edges.

Fold

4 Center rod pocket on back of wall hanging, aligning top cut edges, before adding the binding. Baste in place.

5 Bind edges as detailed at left. After binding is completed, roll back the folded edge of the rod pocket ¼"–½", exposing the "back side" of the pocket. Finger press. Pin the finger pressed fold to the backing fabric.

6 Hand stitch along the pinned fold, catching only a single layer of fabric.

French Twist Binding

This technique, developed by Gretchen Hudock, is a great timesaver! It's an adaptation of the general binding instructions on pp. 136–137, but finishes the quilt edges and creates a rod pocket at the same time. The major difference: The binding is cut wider than with the previous technique.

1 Cut crosswise binding strips 5" wide. The wider strip width provides enough room for inserting a hanger, dowel, or rod after the wall hanging is completed.

2 Join binding strips, right sides together, using diagonal seams to reduce bulk. Fold joined strips in half, wrong sides together, meeting lengthwise edges. Press.

3 Mark the right side of the project ¼" from each corner. Stitch the binding to the wall hanging as indicated in the general instructions, step 3, on p. 136.

4 Press the binding away from the wall hanging on all four sides.

5 Fold the binding on the two side edges to the back of the wall hanging, wrapping the binding around the seam allowances. Pin in place.

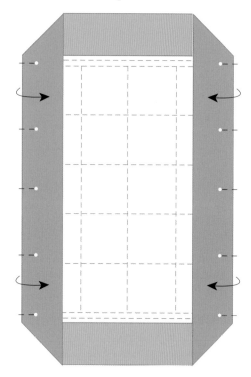

6 Fold top and bottom bindings to the back, tucking in the corners to form miters; pin.

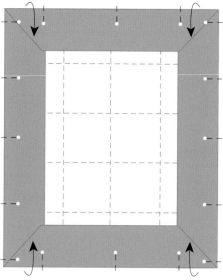

7 Stitch in the ditch, sewing along the seamline on the front of the wall hanging where the binding joins the wall hanging.

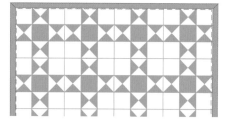

8 Hand stitch side edges of the binding to the back of the wall hanging. Then stitch top and bottom edges to the back of the wall hanging, forming the rod pocket.

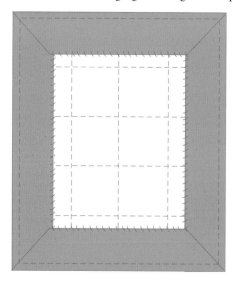

Labels

You have created an heirloom! It's important that you label your quilt. Sign and date it so that it will be part of your family history.

There are many ways to make labels. One alternative is to use a permanent fabric marker, such a Pigma Pen, to sign the back or front of your quilt. Or, here are some other popular label options:

1 **Photocopy labels:** Photocopy a label you have drawn or one of the labels on the following pages. Print the label on an inkjet fabric sheet. Cut out the label, sign it with a permanent fabric marker, and fuse or sew the label to the back of your quilt.

2 **Embroidered labels:** Find your favorite embroidered label design or create your own with built-in frames on your embroidery machine. Use embroidery software to sign your label; fuse or sew the label to the back of your quilt.

3 **Premade purchased labels:** Purchase ready-made labels. Simply sign them with your favorite permanent fabric markers or embroider on them. Fuse or sew these purchased labels to the back of your quilt.

4 **Computer generated labels:** Use your computer to create and sign a label. Print the labels on inkjet fabric sheets. Cut out and fuse or sew the label to the back of your quilt.

Note from Nancy

The following pages include several labels suitable for photocopying onto inkjet fabric sheets. Fuse or sew a label to the back of your quilt. Use a permanent marker to fill in your information.

Quilted with love by

Date _____

Quilted with love by

Date _____

Quilted with love by

Date _____

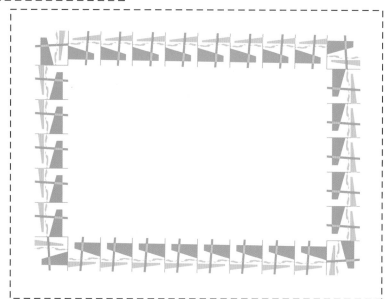

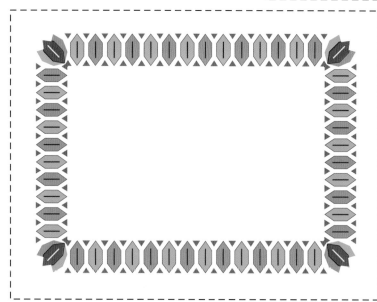

Created with love by

Date _____

Created with love by

Date _____

Glossary

Backing: The pieced or solid fabric that forms the bottom layer of a quilt.

Bartack: A sewing machine zigzag stitch used to secure layers together, with stitch length usually set at "0" and stitch width varying, depending upon the project.

Basting: Long stitches sewn by hand or machine that temporarily hold fabric together. Basting can also refer to pinning or using spray adhesive to hold layers together.

Batting: The lofty middle layer of a quilt that provides warmth and adds depth to a quilt design.

Bearding: When batting fibers emerge through the quilt top or bottom.

Bias: True bias forms a 45° angle to the lengthwise and crosswise threads in a fabric.

Binding: Fabric strips that are folded and sewn to the edge of a project to finish the edge.

Borders: Strips of fabric added to the pieced top of a project to frame it, to add color, or to increase size.

Chain Stitching: Sewing blocks or strips together in a continuous fashion with a chain of stitches between them to save time when quilting.

Cornerstones: Solid or pieced blocks of fabric added to the corners of a quilt, attached to the borders or sashing for added color and design.

Echo Quilting: A method of quilting in which you stitch about ¼" from the pieced or appliquéd design and then continue to echo that stitching in ¼" increments that move outward.

Fat Eighth: A quarter yard of fabric cut in half to measure 9" x 22" instead of the typical ⅛ yd. that measures 4½" x 44". Or, some prefer an 11" x 18" cut of fabric. Both equal the same number of square inches.

Fat Quarter: A half yard of fabric cut in half to measure 18" x 22" instead of the usual ¼ yd. that measures 9" x 44".

Feed Dogs: The grooved metal teeth under the presser foot on a sewing machine that gently grip and move the fabric forward.

Fusible Web: A thin layer of man-made fibers that will melt and bond two layers of fabric with the heat of an iron.

Grainline: Threads in a fabric running in the lengthwise direction. Also referred to as the warp threads in the weaving process.

Grid Line Quilting: Machine quilting in straight lines spaced uniformly vertically, horizontally, or diagonally to form a grid.

Half-Square Triangles: Formed by stitching two squares together diagonally and cutting them apart on the diagonal to yield two half-square triangles.

Hue: Another name for a color.

Intensity: The brightness or dullness of a color.

Layering: Placing two or more layers together for the purpose of quilting. Generally a quilt top, batting, and quilt bottom are layered for a quilt, but if you use flannel or another fabric with loft for one of the layers you may be able to eliminate the batting.

Loft: The thickness of a batting.

Longarm Quilting Machine: A quilting machine that can handle a large quilt to stitch a design that holds the quilt layers together.

Miter: A diagonal seam (45° angle) formed in a corner. In quilting, corners of borders and the binding are often mitered.

Muslin: A simple cotton fabric that has not been overly processed. It can be purchased in its natural cream color with small cotton seed flecks or it can be purchased bleached. It is a very economical substitute for quilting fabric used on the backs of wall hangings, table runners, and more.

On-Point: When quilt blocks are sewn together in diagonal rows, with sides of the blocks at a 45° angle to the sides of the quilt. On-point settings require the addition of setting triangles and corner triangles.

Piecing: Sewing smaller pieces of fabric together to form blocks for a patchwork project.

Presser Foot: The part of a sewing machine that holds the fabric in place as you sew. The edge of a presser foot can be used as a stitching guide to achieve straight seams.

Prewashing: Laundering fabric before it is sewn.

Quarter-Square Triangles: Formed by joining two half-square triangle blocks with a diagonal seam stitched from the opposite corners of the first seams, and then cutting the blocks apart on that diagonal to yield four quarter-square triangles.

Quilt: The result of fabric and batting layered together and stitched or tied to hold the layers together.

Quilt Frame: A frame or hoop to which a quilt is attached for quilting the layers together.

Quilting: The process of piecing fabrics together to make a quilt.

Quilt Label: A label that is usually attached to the back of a quilt to identify the quilter, date, occasion, and/or other pertinent information.

Quilt Sandwich: The quilt top, batting, and backing—layers that make up a quilt.

Rod Pocket: A tube fastened to the top of a quilt back to fit a rod or hanger that will hold a quilted hanging on the wall.

Rotary Cutter and Mat: A sharp cutting tool with a rotary blade used in combination with a straight edge quilting ruler and self-healing mat to cut quilt fabric, strips, blocks, and so forth, during the quilting process. Cut through one or more layers of fabric with ease.

Sashing: The strips of fabric, plain or pieced, used between blocks to increase size, separate designs, add color, and give the quilt pizzazz.

Seam Allowance: The distance from the stitching line to the cut edge of seamed fabrics. The most common seam allowance for quilting is ¼".

Selvages: The woven edges on fabric, running the length of the fabric, parallel to the lengthwise grainline.

Setting Triangles: Used to complete the outer edges of quilt blocks that have been set on-point.

Shades: Colors to which black has been added in varying degrees.

Stash: A term used to describe a sewer's fabric collection.

Stencils: Designs that are usually die cut in plastic template material and traced onto a quilt or blocks before stitching.

Stitch in the Ditch: Stitching on the front of a quilt in the well created by the seam to hold layers together. The stitching is virtually invisible.

Strata: Fabric strips sewn together in the piecing process.

Strip Piecing: A timesaving quilting method involving sewing strips together into strata and then cutting them into sections instead of cutting and sewing each small piece for a section separately.

Squaring: The process of using a square ruler or T-square on quilts or quilt blocks to make sure they are the same measurement vertically, horizontally, and diagonally.

Tint: A color to which white has been added in varying degrees.

Tying: An option for quilting the layers of a quilt together. Usually yarn or floss is used to tie a quilt at intervals or between blocks.

Value: The lightness or darkness of a color.

Walking Foot: Used to feed fabrics evenly when sewing multiple fabric layers. The teeth on the bottom of a walking foot firmly feed the top fabric precisely as the feed dogs move the bottom layer to eliminate shifting.

Strengthen Your Stitching Skills

Quilt As Desired
*Your Guide to Straight-Line and
Free-Motion Quilting*
by Charlene C. Frable

Take your quilting skills to new
heights with the six projects,
using straight-line and free-
motion techniques, featured in
this revolutionary new guide.
Discover what it means to truly
quilt as desired.

Hardcover • 8¼ x 10⅞ • 128 pages
150 color photos
Item# Z0743 • $24.99

Quilting
The Complete Guide
by Darlene Zimmerman

Everything you need to know to
quilt is in this book. More than
400 color photos and illustrations
demonstrating the quilt making
process.

Hardcover • 5⅝ x 7⅞ • 256 pages
400 color photos and illus.
Item# Z0320 • $29.99

Fat Quarter Fun
by Karen Snyder

Indulge in the guilty pleasure
of fat quarter quilts and you'll
be glad you did, with 150
step-by-step photos, and 15+
projects, you'll find countless
ways to have bundles of fun.

Softcover • 8¼ x 10⅞ • 128 pages
75 b&w illus. • 150 color photos
Item# Z0934 • $22.99

The Art of Landscape Quilting
by Nancy Zieman and Natalie Sewell

This one-stop guide includes instructions for 16
upscale step-by-step projects and 20 partial projects;
complete with tips, tricks and techniques for suc-
cessfully designing and completing landscape quilts.

Softcover • 10 x 7 • 144 pages
200 color photos
Item# LCQG • $24.99

Sew with Confidence
*A Beginner's Guide
to Basic Sewing*
by Nancy Zieman

Teaches basic sewing techniques
and provides information on
materials and tools needed to
get started, sewing and serger
machines, organizing the sewing
area, patterns, fabrics and more.

Softcover • 8¼ x 10⅞ • 128 pages
150 color photos, 100 illus.
Item# SWWC • $21.99